# Here Is the Answer

# Here Is the Answer

Godfrey C. Robinson
Stephen F. Winward

Judson Press, Valley Forge

230
R

HERE IS THE ANSWER

# Preface to the American Edition

In the seventies many people are asking whether the Christian faith is still credible in the light of technological progress on the one hand and the many unsolved problems of human relations on the other. However, questions and doubts about Christian belief are not new. For many years people have been asking questions such as: What is the purpose of the world? What is wrong with the world? Are decency and sincerity enough? Has science disproved religion? Answers to these and other questions are given in this book which we are privileged to offer to American readers for the first time. The book has been of great help to readers in Great Britain. In fact, it has been so popular that it has gone through twelve printings by its British publisher.

The authors have chosen several of the most often asked questions about the Christian faith and have answered them in a sympathetic, common sense fashion. Their answers will be satisfying to many readers, and as F. F. Bruce has written on the cover of the original edition, "If in indicating what the Christian answer is they give rise to further questions, that is all to the good."

Stephen F. Winward is coauthor of *Orders and Prayers for Church Worship* which has been accorded a very warm reception by free churchmen in the United States. Among other books which he has written, Dr. Winward has collaborated with Godfrey C. Robinson on a number of titles, some of which are already known to the American reading public.

Judson Press is very glad to be able to introduce this work of these two men who have so effectively combined the abilities of pastor and author.

# Contents

# Preface

A great many people are concerned about the problem of Christian living. But Christian living springs from Christian conviction. Therefore, this book pertains to those beliefs and reliances upon which Christian conduct rests. We have not attempted any kind of systematic exposition of the Christian faith, as there are many excellent books, both large and small, which do that. Experience has shown that there are a number of stock difficulties and objections to Christianity which crop up again and again. These are the questions which we have set ourselves to answer. We have aimed, therefore, not at an academic statement of Christian belief, but rather at a series of chapters dealing with the problems and perplexities of our own day.

Our purpose in this book is threefold. We want first of all to help the Christian to a fuller understanding of his faith. It is often said, with some truth, that whereas the average Communist can give a clear and convincing account of his ideology, the average Christian is vague and uncertain.

There is a widespread need today for instructed Christians. Next, we have endeavored to help the Christian who desires to present a reasoned statement of what he believes to non-Christians. These two purposes are, of course, very closely related—propagation depends upon conviction.

Chiefly, however, we have in mind those who are not convinced Christians, who have not yet begun to walk the Christian way. For many "the way" is blocked with genuine intellectual difficulties, doubts, and perplexities. We appreciate that the removal of intellectual difficulties does not in itself make disciples, but such removal is often a necessary preliminary; it is noteworthy that the apostles themselves were frequently found "reasoning" with their hearers.

There are few people so exasperating as those "who know all the answers," and the authors make no claim to omniscience! There is no complete answer to many of the great questions of life, and the highest wisdom will often consist of the conviction "I know that I do not know." We are not, however, without light on many of the greatest problems; in particular, it is not difficult to expose the fallacies and prejudices in the arguments of many unbelievers. It is high time we began to doubt the doubters; the faith of many people in unbelief needs to be undermined! On the positive side, there is a Christian answer to our deepest problems, and that this answer is constructive, reasonable, and satisfying can be demonstrated.

We acknowledge our debt to F. F. Bruce, M.A., Head of the Department of Biblical Studies in Sheffield University, who has been kind enough to read the manuscript and suggest alterations and improvements. Mr. Bruce is not to be held responsible for any imperfections that remain, but these are less than they would have been apart from his expert advice. Many of the chapters have already appeared in print, but they have been revised for this present volume.

The quotations from the Bible, except where otherwise stated, are from the Revised Standard Version.

It is our sincere prayer that the Spirit of Truth, who graciously makes use of imperfect human work, will use this book to bring seekers to the One who is the only satisfying answer to all the questions and longings of the human heart.                                    G. C. R.

S. F. W.

*The atheist does not believe that God exists. The agnostic says that he does not know and that nothing can be known about God. The Christian claims to know God personally. Who is right? Does God exist, and if so can his existence be proved? What reasons do Christians bring forward to support their conviction that there is a God and that he can be known?*

# 1

## Is There a God?

Proving by reason or logical argument that there is a God is not possible. This should be made quite clear at the outset. It is possible, for example, to prove that the sum of the angles of a triangle is equal to two right angles; but that is only because we are allowed to assume certain truths before starting the theorem. These "axioms" upon which all scientific knowledge rests are acts of faith; that is, self-evident assumptions which cannot be proved. Scientific knowledge, therefore, like religious knowledge, rests upon a foundation of faith. But obviously, in the case of God, we cannot be "given" anything more ultimate than God on which to base the logical proof of his existence. The existence of God himself is the ultimate, the axiom, the ground of all thought, and we have to begin reasoning with this self-evident assumption, this act of faith. This fact, that all thinking and reason presupposes the existence of God, is known as the *ontological argument* and was first expounded by Anselm of Canterbury in the Middle Ages.

That is why thinkers or philosophers who begin by denying the existence of God are compelled to reintroduce him into their systems under some other name. The living, personal God of the Bible is shown out at the front door, only to be readmitted as the "Absolute," or the "Ground of Existence," or "Unconscious Will," or the "Life Force," or the "Principle of Integration," and so on. Man cannot think, much less live, without God. It should also be noted that if the existence of God could be proved rationally, it would mean the end of all faith. In that case we should be compelled to believe. But God does not will us to believe by compulsion, but by the insight of faith. That is why his existence can never be as tangible and obvious as, say, a bus or the fact that one and one make two. The God of Scripture not only reveals himself, but also hides himself, both in order that he may be sought and also that man might "walk by faith and not by sight."

But although the existence of God cannot be proved, that does not mean there is no *evidence* for our belief in God. Faith is not credulity; it is not "a leap in the dark" —it is based upon facts. What, then, are the facts in human life and experience which may be taken as evidence for the existence of God? Five may be selected because of their outstanding importance.

1. *Nature.* The vast and mysterious universe around us is convincing evidence for the existence of God—so convincing that, as Paul points out, even the most corrupted pagan has read of the existence of God in the open book of nature. "Ever since the creation of the world his invisible nature, namely, his eternal power and deity, has been clearly perceived in the things that have been made" (Romans 1:20). And Paul's statement is true to fact; practically all pagans do believe in the existence of a Creator and Sovereign Ruler of the universe.

That the world cannot have issued out of nothing and "that what is seen was made out of things which do not appear" (Hebrews 11:3) is self-evident to the average mind. There must be an ultimate ground of all existence, an uncaused cause, an "unmoved mover," from whose creative activity all existence has issued and is still held in being. Several of our famous contemporary astronomers on the ground of scientific knowledge have pointed out that the universe must have had a definite beginning in time; it is not eternal. If, then, it came into being at a definite time (and the second law of thermodynamics, which teaches that cyclic universes are impossible in the same way as perpetual motion machines are impossible, alone requires this), it must have issued from some ultimate ground and cause, since something cannot come from nothing. It was, in fact, created by the Creator.

This *cosmological argument* is powerfully reinforced by the *teleological argument,* the argument relating to design and purpose. There are unmistakable signs of design throughout the universe, and they are most evident in the kingdom of life. How perfectly everything fits into its environment; how exquisitely perfect is the functioning of all the organs of the body! If there is no Designer, what is the alternative? The spider's web, the human eye, the star-spangled heavens, the mind of man—these are all due to "a fortuitous concourse of atoms"! But design is evident not only in the parts: a great purpose seems to be moving toward some "end" (Greek *telos,* hence *teleological*). There is "one far-off divine event to which the whole creation moves." (Compare Romans 8:18-22.)

2. *Conscience.* The philosopher Kant declared that two things filled him with ever-increasing wonder and awe: "the starry heavens above, and the moral law within" (see Psalm 19). If the existence of God is written in nature, still more is

his eternal moral law written in human nature. All men have this inborn sense of right and wrong, and "show that what the law requires is written on their hearts, while their conscience also bears witness" (Romans 2:15). This sense of obligation or duty, this "categorical imperative," is extremely powerful and persistent, as may be seen in the experience of remorse and guilt. Attempts to explain away this sense of duty as tribal custom, racial habit, social convention, are sheer evasions of the facts, for we all know from within, directly, instinctively, that "I am accustomed" is not the same as "I ought." In any case, how could Jeremiah the prophet (to take one example) have withstood the social conventions of his age in the name of God and his law if the sense of right is simply the product of social custom? The pioneers of right are precisely those who have withstood racial habits and social conventions! This moral consciousness of man must have a source higher than itself; if man feels "I ought," there must be One who says "thou shalt."

3. *Religion*. When the apostle Paul visited Athens, he observed that even the pagans of that city were "very religious," and went on to say that God had created all men "that they should seek God, in the hope that they might feel after him and find him." It is significant that men of all races and in all ages have been "most religious," as the great world religions with all their varieties of belief and practice testify. As Martin Luther said, "Man must have God or an idol." Modern unbelievers, by getting rid of God, simply introduce the "ersatz" or substitute god, the idol. They do not cease to be religious, for man must give supreme devotion to something. Why must man have a god of some kind? Why this universal hunger after the unseen? Is it reasonable to suppose that there is no satisfaction of this universal longing? Is there any other example of a persistent and universal desire, with no corresponding

object of satisfaction? For hunger there is food, for curiosity there is truth—for man there is God.

4. *History.* Much may be learned from the stirring story of the human race in general, especially concerning the inevitable punishment of evil. Here the divine footsteps may often be traced in retribution, in justice, and in judgment, as we have seen in the recent history of Europe. But even to a man with no religious beliefs, the story of one particular race is astonishing. How do we account for Israel? For her existence and career *is a fact* even to a pagan. Why did this small race, passing successively under the domination of several foreign empires, survive? How did she come to possess a moral law without parallel elsewhere? How was she able to produce such remarkable men? How can we account for that unique collection of writings—of history, law, poetry, wisdom, biography, prophecy—which has spoken to the hearts of men in all ages? The contribution of ancient Israel to the history of mankind is unique and is explicable only by the fact that this race was especially chosen by God in working out his purpose for all mankind.

5. *Christ.* The existence of Jesus Christ is likewise a fact of history. How, then, do we account for that fact? No one has, of course, the right to answer this question, unless he has exposed himself to that fact. Read sincerely the teaching of Jesus and the story of his deeds; look at the character depicted in the Gospel story, and observe the manner of his death. Listen to what he says about himself, and to the testimony of many eye-witnesses concerning his resurrection. What, then, do we make of Christ? It is really quite absurd to say that he was a very good man, the best of all men, the flower of humanity, for if he was only that, then he was a deluded fanatic. For clearly he did not regard himself in that light. The only other

possible conclusion is that of the New Testament, "You are the Christ, the Son of the living God." This is, of course, a confession of faith, and as we said at the beginning, we can only know God through faith. But faith is based on fact; it is insight, seeing into the meaning of events. It is in the fact of Christ that God meets man personally. In nature is his hand, in history his footsteps; but in Christ we see his face. To those who have met him the question, "Is there a God?" is replaced by the confident confession, "My Lord and my God!"

*To many people life seems to be meaningless. Is it, in the poet's words, merely "a tale told by an idiot, full of sound and fury, signifying nothing"? We know that we live on a globe spinning in space, peopled by millions of men and women. Is this great universe governed by a definite purpose? If so, what is that purpose, and how does it affect society in general and my life in particular?*

# 2

# What Is the Purpose of the World?

If the world as a whole were without purpose, then each human life would indeed be "a tale told by an idiot, full of sound and fury, signifying nothing." For the life of the individual and of society can only be with purpose if there is a plan for the world as a whole. The part cannot be purposive if the whole is meaningless. Is there, then, such a cosmic purpose?

This question has been answered partly in the first chapter, "Is There a God?" If there is no God, there cannot, of course, be a cosmic purpose, for purpose is a meaningless term apart from personality. A purpose is an end visualized by a mind; and so, no universal mind, no universal purpose. But if there is a God, a living God, who thinks and wills and acts, there must be a universal purpose. Christians claim that this divine purpose for the whole universe was disclosed in Jesus Christ, who came into this world not only to reveal that purpose, but also to achieve it. What, then, is this purpose? That is not an academic but a vital question for us all, for unless we have some knowledge of it, we shall be unable to cooperate with God in its fulfillment.

In attempting a description of this purpose, it may be helpful to take the analogy of artistic creation. Why did Beethoven create his Fifth Symphony, or why did Michelangelo paint his famous picture of Adam? We can only say that it is the very *nature* of the artist to create, and that he finds his highest joy in creative activity. Indeed, this is true not only of the artist, for all personality is by nature creative. Furthermore, the artist himself is revealed in his work, which is the expression and embodiment of his personality. The visitor to St. Paul's Cathedral in London, searching for a memorial to its architect, is directed wisely to look around him. There is likewise in the artist not only the impulse to create and reveal, but also thereby to share with others, to communicate his vision.

Now, all human illustrations have severe limitations when applied to God, and we must not forget the prophetic warning, "To whom then will you compare me? . . . says the Holy One" (Isaiah 40:25). But if we remember this, the illustrations can be most illuminating. The Lord Jesus himself used such a method, proceeding from man to God with the important qualifying phrase "how much more" (see Matthew 7:7-12). In likening God to the artist we must never forget the "how much more." As with the artist, it is of the very nature of God to create. That is the first truth the Bible reveals about him, "In the beginning God created." So also the Apostles' Creed begins with this primary truth, "I believe in God the Father Almighty, Maker of heaven and earth." Like the artist, God finds his supreme joy in creative activity; as it is finely expressed in Scripture, "When I laid the foundation of the earth . . . when the morning stars sang together, and all the sons of God shouted for joy" (Job 38:4, 7; compare Genesis 1:31; Psalm 65:12-13).

Again, like the artist (but "how much more"), God is revealed in his creative work: "The heavens are telling the glory of God; and the firmament proclaims his handiwork" (Psalm 19; compare Psalm 8; Psalm 104; Romans 1:20), and it is a sphere through which he imparts himself to man in many ways, sharing his life and joy with his creatures. The world, then, is the realm of God's creative and revealing activity, and its purpose is his joy and glory (God's glory is his revealed nature): joy which springs from giving, glory from love. "Thou didst create all things and by thy will they existed and were created" (Revelation 4:11). We are aware that that leaves the whole question of suffering in the world to be faced, because so much suffering appears to be unnecessary and gratuitous. That subject is by itself so large and so important we have devoted a special chapter to it later in the book (chapter 17, "Why Does God Permit Suffering?").

To proceed further, God had one special object in creation, one being in whom his own nature could be expressed and revealed in a unique way. For while stars, oceans, flowers, and animals all reveal the divine nature and declare the divine glory, they do so in a very limited way. God's purpose was to create one creature after his "own image and likeness"; that is a person, free, rational, and spiritual. This is the climax of God's creative activity: "Let us make man." But the creation of a person is a vastly more difficult and awful undertaking than the creation of a star or a lion, for in this case the creature himself must cooperate in the undertaking, embracing by free choice the divine purpose and obeying the divine will.

Man has notoriously failed to do that. But it must be made clear that God's purpose was not defeated (even temporarily) by the fall, and the gospel was not a saving afterthought on God's part, but something conceived eternally in the counsel of his will. When a man accepts Christ for himself and becomes a Christian, God's will and purpose are seen at work. What God is after in the world is character, and not just character, but Christlike character. Rightly has the poet said that the world is "a vale of soul-making." The main purpose of the discipline of life is that we should each one become like God. And that means become like Christ, since the Lord Jesus Christ is God manifest in the flesh. With deep simplicity this world purpose of God is expressed by the apostle Paul in two sentences: "Until Christ be formed in you" (Galatians 4:19); "According to his purpose . . . to be conformed to the image of his Son" (Romans 8:28-29). No man is really within the purpose of God unless he is becoming like Christ.

But that is not all. The purpose of God is not just to create a number (even a very large number) of Christlike persons to share his nature and his love. He wills rather to create a community of such beings. His intention is that all personal beings shall be in perfect fellowship with himself and with one another through Jesus Christ.

That is to say, God's purpose is to create a family in which we shall both know and obey him as Father and love one another as brothers. In the New Testament there are several metaphors or pictures of this corporate life which are far more suggestive than a multitude of words. Jesus Christ claims to be the vine, and his followers are the branches, all sharing in the same divine life, and obeying the law of mutual love. Paul speaks of the Body of Christ in which believers are members, having differing functions, yet sharing in a common life. All these illustrations make it clear that God intends us to be *together* in Christ, who has come to break down all barriers between man and man and to make us all one in him. We can express this another way by saying that it is the purpose of God to create the church, the community of those who trust, love, and obey him. Through the church he purposes to make known his love to all personal beings and draw them, if they will respond, into Christ and his community. In the last book of the Bible we see this purpose brought to its fulfillment and fruition. We see there in vision the redeemed and perfected community, the Holy City. That is the end, the fulfillment of the divine purpose.

What a majestic plan! The whole created universe is to reflect the divine nature and be the realm of God's self-giving. God wills to bring "many sons unto glory," making men like Jesus Christ. He purposes to unite all together "in the mystical Body of His Son."

But what does this purpose mean stated in personal terms for each one of us? Just this. God's purpose for me is that everyday I should become more and more like Jesus Christ until I bear his perfect likeness in the world to come. He intends me to be a vital member of the church of Christ, sharing in her worship, fellowship, and work. I am to press to instill these same two purposes in the lives of others, seeking by life and word to bring them into Christ and his church.

Finely summed up in the first article of the Westminster Shorter Catechism, this majestic plan is: "Man's chief end is to glorify God, and to enjoy him for ever." "Unto him are all things." The purpose of the world is—God.

*There may be nothing wrong with the world as it is. Perhaps some people would not have it otherwise. Yet the wars of this century have raised for many of us these awful questions: Is this the world as it ought to be? Why is there so much evil and cruelty, so much strife and frustration? And why do we as individuals find it so hard to do what we know to be right and so easy to do the wrong? What is the basic trouble?*

# 3

## What Is Wrong with the World?

Perhaps we are begging the question. Is there agreement, first of all, that there is *something wrong* with the world? The prior question must be disposed of before we are in a position to investigate the exact nature of the trouble.

To begin with, therefore, we propose to invite into the witness-box four principal sources of evidence: history, literature, law, and conscience. Whatever his religious views may happen to be, or even assuming that he makes no claim to any religious views at all, the average individual today, as he looks out upon the world, is convinced that there is something seriously wrong somewhere. The devastation, material and moral, resulting from all of the wars, large and small, leaves a sorry picture. The fighting ends, but hatreds and suspicions remain. Yet nobody really wants these things— they just happen.

The record of history is that they always have happened. Outward circumstances have, of course, changed with the changing years, but the pages of history vary little in their story of cruelty, want, and war all down the ages. Since the beginning there has been this one continual story of misery and wrong.

Akin to the witness of history is that of the world's literature. For great literature is a mirror of human life, portraying man as he actually is; and the revelation is almost invariably one of human sin and guilt. Whether we look back at the Greek tragedies of ancient days, or at the more recent tragedies of Shakespeare; whether we read the novels of Thomas Hardy the Englishman, or of Dostoevski the Russian, this ugly fact is seen portrayed. And we sense that the portrayal is true to life. To what conclusion about human nature are we led by the amazing insight of our greatest English poet and dramatist? Something is obviously wrong with a world where situations arise such as those depicted in *Othello* or *King Lear*.

There is the further evidence of law. A great part of the legislation produced by every society or nation is an elaborate attempt to restrain and punish what is admitted to be a fact, man's wrongdoing. This attempt to enforce right conduct and to restrain wrong conduct, which we call law, is, by its very existence, a universal testimony to the fact of human evil.

Lastly, we know that the witness of conscience in private and personal matters confirms the evidence already brought forward. In the smaller world of our own circumstances we experience personal "wrongs" and domestic tragedies. Why are we unable to do those things that we know to be right, and why do we find ourselves committing actions which in our better moments we despise? Our own inner experience is in full agreement with the testimony of a great writer, which is all the more remarkable in that he was also a great saint: "For I do not do the good that I want but the evil I do not want is what I do. . . . I find it to be a

law that when I want to do right, evil lies close at hand. . . .
Wretched man that I am!" (Romans 7:19, 21, 24).

We are now in a position to put the original question,
and there is found no lack of proffered answers. Some of
them can be dismissed quickly: ancient superstitions, for
example, that the "gods" were evilly disposed toward men.
The primitive man who lives in terror of animistic and spirit
enemies stirs our sympathy and deserves our help, but he
cannot lay claim to an adequate explanation of evil.

The suggestions of some of the ancient philosophies are,
however, deserving of notice. Among the Greeks there were
those who taught that matter itself was evil. Sin was therefore rooted in the body and its passions. In the form of various Gnostic heresies these views were held by many who
claimed to be members of the Christian church in the early
centuries of the faith. It became necessary, of course, to
postulate two gods in order to explain creation: God himself
was the fount of goodness, but there was also an inferior
deity (called the Demiurge) who made the material world
which was evil. Hindu philosophy has attempted to explain,
or rather explain away, evil with its doctrine of *maya* or
illusion, by which the world of sense is dismissed as unreal.
Are there echoes of this attempt to evade the facts in the far
more recent doctrines of Christian Science?

Much of the present ignorance concerning the true nature
of evil, and much of the blame for the attitude of mind
which regards the Bible doctrine of sin as hopelessly out
of date, must be laid at the door of the modern evolutionary
conception of history. Men came to accept the nineteenth-
century illusion that the world was getting better and better
through the working of some automatic process; the golden
age was just around the corner. Hence the popularity of
such phrases as "The *upward* march of mankind" and "The
*progress* of civilization," the words in italics in both cases

being very much open to question. The "explanation" of evil which evolution has to offer is that the instincts and passions of a lower stage of development tend to persist and override the more recently developed reason and moral sense. Sin is therefore an anachronism, a kind of moral hangover. Eventually it will pass. But we look around us—and wonder!

The most popular view today perhaps is that, while the reality of evil is admitted, it is likewise asserted that man can save himself. The ancients used to say that the flesh was evil. They were wrong, we are now told: it is the mind. Hence comes the modern version of humanism—the conception that man can by himself create a new order of society. All that he requires is education; his trouble is not sin, but ignorance. Train his mind and improve his environment, and you have solved his problem; statements such as these are familiar to those who have listened to modern Communist propaganda.

If all this is true and education alone is needed, then university students ought to be outstanding for their moral qualities, noticeably better than anybody else. Is it a fact that a trained mind means a better character? The training of the mind, as of the body, is an excellent thing, but should never be confused with a transformation of nature. Observation of the last few decades reveals that one of the apparent effects of education has been to turn devils into clever devils. It is against the evidence to say that man can save himself. Why has he not done so before now, for he has made many attempts?

Now, sin is a disease and, like some other diseases, results not only in blindness but also in paralysis. When it reaches an acute form, the sufferer tends to be unaware of its existence. A time came in the life of Damien, the great missionary to the lepers, when he accidentally poured a pot of boiling water over his foot and discovered with horror that he felt no pain. Not before that moment had he realized that he himself was leprous. The situation confronting us today is that of a world suffering from the ravages of sin in an advanced form. That is why there is so little awareness of the reality of sin. But what is meant by the word "sin"?

It is taught in Scripture that man *was created in perfection* to be a child of God, that he *is now a fallen creature,* but that he *can be restored* through Christ. The account of this fall in Genesis 3 gives us the truth in a nutshell. If outside corroboration is required, then here is the statement of an archeologist, who writes: "In my opinion, the history of the oldest religion of man is a rapid decline from monotheism to extreme polytheism and widespread belief in evil spirits. It is in a very true sense the history of the fall of man." Man was created in the image of God; that is to say, he is a personal being, possessing freedom of choice, reason, and other spiritual qualities. But he misused this freedom, under diabolical influences, to rebel against God: the whole world is now in a state of revolt. This fact must be grasped firmly. Sin is more than a fact or an act; it is a fixed attitude toward God.

Thus it is the human will which has become perverted and sinful. Man, who is *by nature* dependent, has sought to be independent. Man, who is *by nature* a creature, has chosen to be his own god. "You will be like God," said the tempter. This display of human arrogance and self-sufficiency is perfectly illustrated by our Lord's story of the prodigal son. The sin of the son was his attitude to his father, his rebellion against his authority and love, his desire to live in independence of him, resulting in the separation in a far country. Could there be a simpler, and yet more accurate, picture of the state of the world today?

The malady is therefore centered in the will and results

in the darkening of the mind and the perversion of the passions. This is what the Bible means when it says that the *heart* of man, and not merely his head, is wrong. In Hebrew thought the heart is first of all the seat of volition, or the will. Those Greeks were too superficial who taught, what is still held by some today, that sin is sensuality arising from the body and its passions. Admittedly these have been made the instruments of sin, but the perverted will is the basic trouble. *I myself am a sinner.* G. K. Chesterton was right when he met the question, "What is wrong?" with the answer, "I am wrong!"

Yet his answer was incomplete. The assertion that evil is rooted in the hearts of individuals has a complementary truth in the fact that sin also manifests and embodies itself in our corporate life and institutions. There is a racial fall and a kingdom of evil. So we are compelled to recognize not only that "I am wrong," but also that "we are wrong," since sin, which in the first instance is personal, gets caught up into human society and institutions and thus perpetuates itself with frightful and fatal power in the lives of other individuals.

The victory of Christ will not neglect this racial aspect. That is why Christ died for *the world,* effecting a racial redemption and creating a new redeemed humanity. It will be part of our Lord's final triumph to effect that deliverance. "The creation itself will be set free from its bondage to decay and obtain the glorious liberty of the children of God. We know that the whole creation has been groaning in travail together until now" (Romans 8:21-22).

*Scientists tell us that the world must end sometime. But how will it end? Perhaps we wonder whether nuclear war will destroy the civilization we have known. Should we give heed to these alarmist rumors and believe that our world is hastening rapidly to destruction? Or dare we be more optimistic and hope that things will gradually get better and better? Have recent events been but the birth pangs of some wonderful new order?*

# 4

## How Will the World End?

Since the dropping of the atomic bomb on Hiroshima in August, 1945, everybody has felt more than ever uncertain about the future. What is likely to happen to the human race? Are we drifting slowly or rapidly toward another world war, a nuclear war which would result in the destruction of civilization? Is it even possible that man may destroy the planet on which he lives? Or shall we take the more optimistic view that man will be able to control these new discoveries, using them beneficially to abolish disease and want, and so by an ordered progress create a Utopia on earth? Are the alternatives destruction or Utopia, or is there yet a third possibility?

People differ considerably in their answers to "How will the world end?" That the world will end is not, however, an open question. Even the materialist admits this. The sun upon which our planet depends is losing energy in enormous quantities every minute, and eventually (if nothing else happened) life in all its forms would be frozen off the earth.

In this connection, we may point out in passing the inner contradiction of a philosophy such as Communism. For even if the ideal society can be achieved by man on earth, it faces sure and ultimate destruction. Why struggle to achieve that which cannot remain? Or is it, perhaps, worthwhile to achieve Utopia for a time?

But here is a further contradiction. If man achieves his ideal in time, in history, he has then nothing else for which to live, no unrealized aim and no hope. Life would become stagnant. Who would choose *to live* in Plato's Republic? The truth is that only a conviction or faith that life finds its fulfillment outside and beyond our time and this earth can give meaning and purpose to our present history and to this world.

Here let us note that the word "end" may have two meanings. It may mean merely "the finish," as in the sentence "I came to the end of the road." It may also mean "the fulfillment," as when we say "the end of the acorn is the oak tree." Of course, the word may be used in both senses: the end of a book or of a play is not merely the finish, but also that which reveals the whole meaning of all that has gone before, and fulfills it. The Bible uses the word in this full sense. The end of the world (or age) is not merely the finish of things, but the last chapter of the book of time, the final act of the long drama of history which reveals and fulfills all that has gone before. "The end" is "the one far-off [except that it may not now be far off] divine event to which the whole creation moves."

What then is this divine event, this last chapter to which all creation is moving, and in which the stirring story of man finds fulfillment? In the Old Testament the prophets called it "the day of the Lord." They regarded this world as an arena, in which the powers of God and of his kingdom were in constant conflict with the powers of evil. In their age the powers of evil were predominant and enthroned in human lives and institutions, but eventually the prophets believed that God would intervene from the eternal world and establish his kingdom on earth himself.

The good news of the New Testament is the proclamation that this divine intervention has taken place. The "day of the Lord" has already dawned, the kingdom has come and has been established through the life and redeeming work of the Lord Jesus Christ. The Eternal has entered time, and the "last things" are already here. So the apostle Peter, speaking on the day of Pentecost, quoted Joel's prophecy, "And it shall be in the last days," prefaced by the decisive words "*This* is what was spoken by the prophet" (italics added). But although the kingdom came and was established in Christ, it has not yet been fulfilled; it is present but not complete.

But because the kingdom is now present in strength, the struggle between God's kingdom and the powers of darkness goes on in an intensified form. This is the clue to subsequent history. It is not a progress but a conflict. It is an unceasing warfare between the woman, the symbol of the kingdom of God, and "the great red dragon," the symbol of the devil and the powers of darkness (Revelation 12). History is not a progress toward Utopia, for the tares as well as the wheat in the field of the world are growing toward the final crisis of harvest. There is a growth, a maturing of both good and evil in the world, and therefore an intensified conflict leading up to the final crisis when the Lord of the field will return with his sickle to reap.

In the light of this revelation given in Jesus Christ, we can outline the answer to our original question as follows:

1. The earth is an arena and not a Utopia. It will remain such to the end. As long as this world lasts, the powers of the kingdom of God and the kingdom of Satan will be in conflict in human lives, in human societies, and in world history.

Therefore we must not anticipate peace and tranquillity, but strife and conflict. Every generation must fight in this struggle, for there are no mere spectators of the situation.

2. As history moves toward its climax, this conflict will not only continue but will intensify. The struggle will become more and more severe as the issue becomes clearer. Toward the end, the powers of evil will break through all restraint (such as the restraints of civil law and order); and being apparently victorious, the earth will experience "the woes," a series of terrible catastrophes and sufferings leading up to the end.

3. "The end" will come by the visible return of the Lord Jesus Christ in great power and glory. For he is not only the Alpha of this world, being the Word "through whom all things were made"; he is also the Omega, the goal and fulfillment of all creation. Creation is "through him and for him" (Colossians 1:16). Jesus Christ is the clue to world history, its finish, and its fulfillment. In the last act of this great drama Christ will be visibly present. We shall see his face (Revelation 1:7).

At his appearing, the dead will be raised and the living transformed "in the twinkling of an eye" (1 Corinthians 15:52). For of what value is a Utopia in which previous generations (who may have suffered for it) cannot share? We shall be dealing with the question "What happens after death?" in a later chapter. It is sufficient here to state that the kingdom involves resurrection, for it is to include the faithful of all ages. After resurrection comes separation: the tares from the wheat, the sheep from the goats, "for we must all appear before the judgment seat of Christ" (2 Corinthians 5:10).

This, then, is "the end"—Jesus himself. That is why those who know him have already "tasted . . . the powers of the age to come," and have already experienced "the last things." "The earth is the Lord's," and one day the longing prayer of the faithful, "thy kingdom come, on earth," will be turned into the triumphant song. "The kingdom of the world has become the kingdom of our Lord and of his Christ: and he shall reign for ever and ever" (Revelation 11:15).

*The average person finds it hard to picture Jesus Christ as a real person. Frequently at the back of our minds is the impression produced by stained-glass windows and religious paintings. If, as Christians claim, Jesus Christ was "God manifest in the flesh," then what was he like? What did he look like? And what is the explanation of the fact that he appealed to all types of men and women?*

# 5

## What Was Jesus Like?

The historical evidence for the existence of Jesus of Nazareth is abundant and impressive, and no reliable historian today would set it aside. The few references which have been made by both pagan and Jewish historians about the life and ministry of Jesus are in general agreement with the accounts of the Christian evangelists. Jesus lived—of that there is little doubt. But many raise the question, "What was he like?"

For many people Jesus Christ is not a real person, although they are prepared to believe that he actually lived. They have received their vague impressions of him from stained-glass windows and religious pictures. Some of these impressions are quite distorted. How often, for example, he is represented exclusively as "gentle Jesus, meek, and mild," ignoring the complementary truth that he was also "the Lion of the tribe of Judah." Since God is revealed in the character of Christ, it is clearly most important to know what he was actually like; another good reason for reading the Gospels in particular and the New Testament in general.

The first page of a modern biography is usually the portrait
of the person about whom the book is written. It seems at first
a little disappointing that we have no such portrait of Jesus.
Not only has no reliable picture of him come down to us,
but the sacred writers give us no verbal description of his
physical appearance. There is no doubt a divine purpose in
this. Such a picture would have concentrated our attention
too much on externals and nonessentials, on the Christ according to the flesh, instead of the contemporary risen Lord.
But although no such description is given, it is clear from
the narrative that the face and looks of Jesus made a profound
impression. "He looked around them with anger" (Mark
3:5). His eyes must have blazed "like a flame of fire" (Revelation 1:14). With a kind but searching glance, "the Lord
turned and looked at Peter" (Luke 22:61). Of the rich young
ruler it is said, "And Jesus looking upon him loved him"
(Mark 10:21). These and other references make it plain that
the eyes and face of Jesus were expressive and revealing;
in the words of Paul: "the light of the knowledge of the glory
of God in the face of Christ" (2 Corinthians 4:6).

But what was the character like, that was revealed in that
face? One despairs of describing it. It is like trying to describe
a sunset or a symphony. In describing an ordinary person
(e.g., in a funeral oration), it is usual to single out certain
characteristic virtues. But this cannot be done with Jesus,
for *all* the virtues are fully present in his character. Every
virtue known to man is characteristic of Jesus. So for this
reason the predominant impression made by his character
is that of *fullness*. To use a word of Paul's, the character of
Christ is "manifold," many-sided, iridescent. It is like a
diamond with a variety of beautiful facets or a rainbow com-
pounded of many lovely colors. It is not very helpful to make
a list of all his graces and virtues, for the rainbow is more
beautiful than the separate colors.

This leads to the observation that the virtues of Jesus are not found in isolation, as is so often the case with us. Rather each virtue is balanced by its opposite or complementary. To give but a few instances: He was compassionate and stern; he was joyful and sorrowful; he was patient and yet often indignant; he was zealous and yet calm; he was humble and assertive; he loved solitude and he loved society; he was mystical and practical. These complementaries might be continued almost indefinitely. The balance is most significant; our virtues often have the defects of their qualities. For example, if a man is zealous, he is apt to be hard and intolerant; if, on the other hand, he is tolerant and kindly, he is apt to lack conviction and purpose. But the virtues of Jesus are never thus found isolated from their complementaries. In him there is a perfect balance of character. He is complete.

Just as the virtues of Jesus cannot be isolated from his character as a whole, neither can his character be isolated from his vocation. Biographers often point out that great character and lofty vocation are inseparable. A man is great *for* something. This is supremely true of Jesus. The dominant passion of his life was the fulfillment of his vocation: "My food is to do the will of him who sent me, and to accomplish his work" (John 4:34). What an intensity of purpose is expressed in the moving words, "I came to cast fire upon the earth; and would that it were already kindled!" (Luke 12:49). The personality of Jesus was aflame with passionate loyalty to God's will and purpose. He lived for the kingdom with zeal and ardor. And so the Lord's virtues are the virtues of his vocation: his faithfulness to the will of God; his courage in the face of his enemies and of danger; his patience with the stupidity and sins of his disciples; his zeal to see the work accomplished; his self-sacrifice in life and death. At no point can the character and the vocation of Jesus be separated.

In others, intensity of conviction and loyalty to vocation often lead to neglect of the social virtues and responsibilities. But with Jesus this was not so. It is truly amazing that one so zealous and so ardent should have discharged so fully all the responsibilities of social life. He was joyful and often ironical and humorous. He loved social life and was considerate and courteous. He welcomed women disciples (an unheard-of thing in those days) and little children. For thirty years he discharged all the obligations of family life and tenderly made provision for his mother as he was dying on the cross (John 19:26-27). True, he sometimes had to be stern with his family, but the loyalty of Mary and the subsequent discipleship and devotion of his brothers James and Jude speak for themselves. He was a great patriot giving his life to show his own people the things which belonged to their peace and weeping tears of grief and tender compassion over the impenitent and doomed Jerusalem (Luke 19:41; compare Matthew 23:37). And how he loved his friends! (John 13:1). But his love was not confined to them, for it embraced all mankind, including his enemies, for whom he prayed as he was nailed to the cross. The goodness of Jesus was both inward and outward, a perfect nature expressed in perfect personal relationships.

Lastly, we must note the amazing vitality of Jesus. We find in him fullness of life and vigor. Here is One who is intensely alive. This amazing vitality is seen in all three aspects of his personality: intellectual, emotional, volitional. His mind was swift and penetrating. Every attempt to catch him by craft or to defeat him in controversy was doomed to failure (see Mark 12:13-40). He thought in vivid pictures, setting forth the truth with simplicity, and yet men have never fathomed the amazing depth of his teaching. His emotional completeness and intensity are not less remarkable. For Jesus was no Stoic cultivating apathy and stifling the emotions. He was moved with compassion at the sight of the leper; with fierce anger he drove the crowd from the temple courts; he sighed in sorrow, wept in grief, and rejoiced in the Holy Spirit. There was a full flow of emotional life. To the strength of his firm and inflexible will we have already referred in connection with his vocation. In what other human being do we find the full and equal development of these three aspects of personality? Again one is impressed by the fullness of Jesus.

From whatever angle one approaches the character of Jesus, it is found to be unique and incomparable. Reading the Gospels, one is soon impressed, as were the first disciples, by his absolute goodness. The absence of defect and flaw rightly lead us to speak of his sinlessness. But "sinlessness" is a negative term; rather what we find in Jesus is something intensely vital and positive, absolute goodness and perfect wholeness. His character alone is a convincing testimony that he is more than man. This absolute truth, this matchless beauty, this perfect goodness is the very life of God disclosed to men. As the apostle Paul says, it was just not possible that death should hold and master such intense life. He burst the bonds of death and lives in the power of an endless life. He is our great Contemporary, living with and within those who trust, obey, and love him, transforming them into this same glorious image and likeness through the Lord, the Spirit.

*I had not been born when Jesus was put to death outside Jerusalem. How then can such a distant event affect my life today, and why should I be interested in it? Admittedly, his death appears to have been both cruel and unjust, but others have died a martyr's noble death. I can feel sorry for Christ and be moved by his example. But how does the cross concern me more than this?*

# 6

## How Does the Cross Concern Me?

That Jesus of Nazareth was put to death by crucifixion over nineteen centuries ago is a fact of history for which there is ample evidence.

Calvary, therefore, was an event within history, at a certain place and at a certain time. Yet not long after that time Christian preachers were proclaiming to their hearers that definite moral and spiritual benefits accrued from that death at Jerusalem and that the responsibility for it reached far beyond the immediate actors in the drama. "Christ died for our sins" was the verdict of the writers of the New Testament. Centuries later a hymn writer could describe the cross as: "The balm of life, the cure of woe . . . The sinner's refuge here below," while another wrote: "In the cross of Christ I glory, tow'ring o'er the wrecks of time." What was it that caused men to write thus of the death of Christ? How can there possibly be any connection between my life today and that life that was offered up so many years ago? In short, how does the cross concern me?

Two observations are necessary by way of further introduction. First, the One who died outside Jerusalem was not just a man, one among many others. We have developed this point (concerning the Person of Jesus Christ) in the previous chapter, but it is important to emphasize here that Jesus of Nazareth was "God manifest in the flesh," and so shared the nature of God the Creator. The action of one individual, however noble, does not affect the entire race. Socrates was a good man and suffered death as a martyr; but he was no more than a man, and his death makes little or no difference to us today. What God, the Creator, the Source of life, has done must, however, have vastly different results.

And second, just as Jesus was more than a man, so we must remember that his sufferings were more than physical. It is sometimes objected that other people in the history of the race have suffered unjustly, often with excruciating pain. Were there not also two thieves suffering death by crucifixion alongside Christ? While we do not minimize the physical sufferings of Jesus, his real passion, although including them, was something infinitely deeper. The awful spiritual agony of One who was perfectly holy, bearing the sin of the whole world (a statement which we will later expand) is entirely beyond all human experience. This agony already is beheld in Gethsemane: He was enduring no physical suffering there, and yet so intense was his anguish that his sweat fell like great drops of blood on the ground.

Having realized that he who died on the cross was not merely a man and that his sufferings were not mainly physical, we may now proceed to inquire why the cross concerns us all. It does so, to begin with, because we all share in the responsibility for it. It is no answer for any one of us to say, "But I was not alive then!" Our sins today make their contribution to the sum total of evil which crucified Jesus. There is a sense in which we sin as individuals; thus a man individually may tell a lie, or wrong a friend, or steal a book. Yet even such statements are an oversimplification. Those same sins have their origin in the common life of mankind; for example, the theft of the book may be linked to the evil influence of other people, or the underpayment of labor, or a warped ambition due to an unfair social system. Man is a social being, and there is a kingdom of evil. Presenting the sins of individuals in isolation is not a true picture.

To take a modern event—who was responsible for the dropping of the atom bomb on Hiroshima? It becomes immediately apparent that we cannot answer, "A few American airmen." The handful of men in the particular plane had a share in the responsibility, but they were no more responsible in the final analysis than any other American or Allied national. That which they did was done *on behalf of* all of us; we are as responsible as they.

So it was on the first Good Friday. The rabble, the Jewish leaders, the Roman authorities, even the traitor Judas, were our representatives. As Dr. James Stewart expresses it: "Let us remember that the evil things which put Jesus on the cross were by no means unfamiliar or abnormal. Self-interest in Caiaphas, fear in Pilate, impurity in Herod, anger and spite in the crowd—these were the things which, coming in contact with the Sinless One, deliberately compassed his death. That is to say, Jesus was crucified by the ordinary sins of every day. We are all in this together. Our heart and conscience tell us, when we stand on Calvary, that what we see there is our own work, and that the sins we so lightly condone result always in the crucifixion of the Son of God. In this sense, to quote a great Christian conception, the Lamb is 'slain from the foundation of the world' (Revelation 13:8, KJV), and still is slain today."

When "God manifest in the flesh," a statement which in itself conveys a great mystery, was put to death through the malice of his enemies outside Jerusalem, the evil which put him there was the focus at a point in time of the sin of the whole world. And in that universe of evil you and I have a part.

But just as we share in the *responsibility,* so also we may share in the *benefits.* An illustration will help us here, although any illustration of an event which was both divine and unique is bound to be less than satisfactory. This illustration derives its force from the fact already mentioned that Christ, the God-Man, who is one in nature with God the Creator, is himself therefore the Source of life.

Our bodies are made up of millions of living cells. If a body is stricken with disease, then one healthy cell alone will not be able to save it. The healing agent must be diffused throughout the body so that every cell will be affected. Then new life and vigor are felt in every part of the body. Socrates, Confucius—each man was one cell. Christ is the life of men, the source of the life of the whole race (see John 1:3), and in his Incarnation he became one with the whole life of men. Thus Jesus was the representative or racial man (as Paul expresses it, "the last Adam"), so that when he died, *all* died with him (2 Corinthians 5:14, "One has died for all; therefore all have died"); and *all* men will be raised through him (1 Corinthians 15:22, "For as in Adam all die, so also in Christ shall all be made alive").

The cross concerns me, therefore, because Jesus was not just a human creature as I am, but the Son of God dealing with the world's fundamental problem of evil. Thus St. Gregory of Nyssa, who lived in the fourth century A.D., described Calvary as an *actus medicinalis,* a healing remedy which God provided to pervade the whole diseased system of humanity. The divine commingled with human nature, so that "where the disease was, there the healing power attended."

Gregory's interpretation was, of course, one among very many. The blessings of the experience have been shared by men right through the centuries, but the ways in which those blessings have been expressed have varied to some extent with the variety of differing backgrounds. The cross effects rebirth into divine sonship, acquittal from the condemnation of the law, release from the dominion of sin and death, the payment of a debt, the lifting of a burden, the awakening of love toward God. All these interpretations are true, and although the fact of redemption itself and our experience of it is greater than all the interpretations, all seek to express a personal experience which no critic without this experience has a right to dispute.

So then Christ, the sinless One, suffered upon the cross. In the responsibility of that death the whole of mankind has a share. As that responsibility is recognized in true *repentance,* and the response which we call *faith* is made to the Lord now risen and alive, it is a simple, yet accurate, statement of what has taken place to sing: "Bearing shame and scoffing rude, in *my place* condemned He stood." As with Bunyan's Christian, it remains true to experience that the cross gives "rest by his sorrow, and life by his death." Calvary is the place where hearts become glad and lightsome, and burdens are rolled away.

An objection is sometimes raised against the morality of vicarious suffering. Our Lord described his death as "a ransom for [instead of] many" (Mark 10:45). But is it right that one should suffer on behalf of another? Leaving aside the most important consideration that the cross was God's appointed way of delivering mankind from evil, it is relevant to point out that vicarious suffering is an integral part of life itself. It is happening all around us; millions in the world today are suffering for the misdeeds of others. A mother's heart may break on account of the wrongdoing of her son. This is all suffering caused through others. God willingly takes suffering upon himself in order to effect redemption. This is an act of pure love and cannot possibly be immoral, since love is itself the fulfillment of the whole moral law.

The question, "Does the cross concern me?" thus leads to a further question, "Why ought I to be concerned about the cross?" It is evident that the fact that Christ died has a vital bearing upon the life which I now live.

In chapter 3, "What Is Wrong with the World?" we drew attention to the reality of sin, showing that the fundamental evil of a wrong relationship with God was the source of all other evils so manifest in the world around us. Before God we are guilty, unrighteous, already condemned. The death of Christ, however, is the action of God himself restoring a right relationship, clearing our guilt, and leading to our acquittal. No *man* ever has conquered, or ever can conquer, sin completely. But Christ, who is uniquely God-man, did conquer; and it is our privilege to share in his conquest. The cross is therefore my only hope against my worst enemy, the only way in which I can be "saved"; and the kind of prayer that is voiced in Toplady's great hymn, "Rock of Ages," faces facts and is an expression of spiritual sanity: "Be of sin the double cure—cleanse me from its guilt and power."

In a great war there is usually one critical battle which decides the ultimate victory. The battle between good and evil has been agelong, but at the cross of Calvary there took place the critical battle against private and cosmic evil. Henceforth the victory is assured, and the choice is with ourselves whether or not we will share in that victory. As we trust in his redeeming blood, we become "more than conquerors through him that loved us."

*It is a stupendous claim that Jesus is no longer dead but that he did actually rise again. Can this, however, be proved? It has been truthfully said that the resurrection is the keystone of the Christian faith. To examine carefully the historical evidence is therefore all the more important. What proof is there that the resurrection did take place and that Jesus is alive at this moment?*

# 7

## Did Jesus Rise from the Dead?

"One Jesus, who was dead, but whom Paul asserted to be alive." Festus, the Roman procurator of Judea, rightly saw that this was the issue between the apostle Paul and the opponents of the Christian faith. Is Jesus Christ dead or alive? There can be no question so momentous as this, for everything depends upon the answer. If he did not rise, then the Christian church is founded upon a myth, and "we are of all men most pitiable." If Jesus Christ did rise, then his whole message and Person are vindicated, and sin and death are vanquished; he is "designated Son of God in power . . . by his resurrection" (Romans 1:4). Just as in the great Crusades, Christians battled with Moslems for the possession of "the Holy Sepulchre," so the real contest between belief and unbelief is always around that empty tomb.

"I know that my Redeemer lives"; but how do I know? That joyful conviction is like a strong rope twisted from four strands. Each strand is strong when taken separately, but it is in their unity that the "sure and certain hope" is found.

In life they always belong together, but in thought we can separate them. These, then, are the four strands.

1. *The testimony of the eyewitnesses.* We depend for our knowledge of any event in the distant past upon those who witnessed it. The eyewitnesses themselves may write down what they saw (primary testimony), or their spoken testimony may be written down by those who heard them (secondary testimony). In the New Testament we have both kinds of testimony to the resurrection of Christ. Matthew the tax collector and John, "the disciple whom Jesus loved," were both companions of Jesus and eyewitnesses of the resurrection, and we have their own written accounts of it. So also the apostle Paul, who saw the risen Lord on the road to Damascus, provides us with primary testimony in his letters. In particular, in his first letter to the church at Corinth, he gives us a list of resurrection appearances (six in number), one of which was to over five hundred people at once, most of whom were still alive when he wrote (1 Corinthians 15:3-8).

John Mark, who was the companion of Peter and wrote down Peter's testimony, and Luke the physician, who received the information from the original "eyewitnesses and ministers of the word," both provide us with secondary testimony.

We have, then, ample written evidence for the resurrection, all the more valuable because it comes from several independent writers. It is interesting to note that there is hardly another event in the distant past for which we have so much written evidence. Let the reader inquire how we know that Julius Caesar landed in Britain in 55 B.C., or that Alexander the Great fought the battle of Issus in 333 B.C., and he will discover how plentiful in comparison is the written evidence for the resurrection.

But granted that we have several written accounts of a very early date, how do we know that these stories are reliable and true? May they not be "cunningly devised fables"? Or even if, perhaps, the writers did not "make the accounts up," may they not have "written them up"? Were the first disciples in fact sincere and sensible men with a respect for truth and fact, or were they either deceivers or deceived? This brings us to our second point.

2. *The experiences of the first disciples.* Let us suppose for a moment that Jesus did not rise. How, then, do we account for the resurrection "myth"? Clearly the body could not have remained in the tomb, or the enemies of Jesus would gladly have produced it to refute the "myth." But perhaps it was stolen by the disciples, who then put the story about that he was risen? This plausible theory, first advanced by the Jews, will scarcely bear investigation. We know from our records that the followers of Jesus were completely broken in spirit by the awful and unexpected tragedy of the crucifixion. They were stunned and in complete despair. Furthermore, having run away from their Master at the hour of his arrest, they were now trembling behind bolted doors "for fear of the Jews." We are asked to believe that this band of broken and dispirited men got together, worked out a clever plot, carried it out successfully, and then at the risk of their own lives persistently announced that he was risen! Do men usually face bitter persecution and even death to proclaim what they know to be a myth?

The theory that these men, so obviously sincere and genuine, would resort to such a fraud is so absurd that it is rarely advanced nowadays. Much more popular is the theory of "subjective visions." As the pagan philosopher Celsus, writing about A.D. 170, put it: "Who beheld the risen Jesus? A half-frantic woman, as you state, or some other person, who had either dreamed so owing to a peculiar state of mind, or under the influence of a wandering imagination, had formed to himself an appearance according to his own wishes." So the appearances were but dreams, hallucinations, projections, telepathic states, or wish-fulfillments. But did Paul the persecutor wish to see the risen Lord? Do over five hundred people at once suffer from hallucinations? Did Thomas the doubter and realist deceive himself by having a vision? Rather, we find the rationalist "explanation" more difficult to believe than the Christian faith.

The transformation of these first disciples is one of the most striking facts in all history. They were terrified: They became as bold as lions. They were in the dungeon of Giant Depair: They were begotten again unto a living hope. Their faith was utterly shattered: They became aflame with conviction. Cowards became heroes, weaklings pillars of strength; doubters were transformed into believers, deserters into apostles. What had brought about this mighty change? What was this event, to testify to which they were prepared to die —and did die? There can be only one answer: *"The Lord is risen indeed."*

3. *The Fact of the Christian Church.* The rise, expansion, and triumphs of the Christian church can be adequately accounted for only in one way: "And they went forth and preached everywhere, while the Lord worked with them" (Mark 16:20). We do not mean to imply by this that the spread and worldwide influence of the Christian ideology or of the Christian ethic is in itself proof that Jesus lives. The rise, rapid expansion, and success of Islam does not prove that Mohammed rose from the dead. There is something unique about the Christian church; and it is not the fact that multitudes believe the doctrine concerning Jesus or regulate their conduct by the ethic of Jesus, but that multitudes of all ages claim to have met Jesus, to know Jesus, to be in fellowship with Jesus, to be "in Christ."

Now, this is a most remarkable fact. Is it possible to believe that millions have been deceived about this? And not only people with a mystical bent, but all types, including men of mighty intellectual power, such as Augustine or Calvin? What a remarkable illusion indeed to "take in" so many people, from every race under the sun, and of every age since Christ. What a remarkable illusion to transform countless lives and act as a perpetual ferment within society. Is not this tremendous story, this continuation of the Acts of the Apostles, a sure sign of the fulfillment of the promise, "Lo, I am with you always"?

4. *Personal Experience.* Now if the testimony of the original eyewitnesses (the New Testament), corroborated in the continuing experience of the Christian church, is true—then Jesus Christ is risen, is "alive forevermore." But if that is the case, then I myself, here and today, can meet him and know him. This is the final "strand." "You ask me how I know he lives—he lives within my heart!" Naturally, this can never be evidence to an unbeliever, since by his very unbelief he is excluded from such an experience. But to any who make the venture of faith, the above quotation is not just a pious cliché, but a great fact.

The life of an individual can be indwelt by the living Lord, can know the pressure of another and greater will upon his own, can feel from within his urge towards love and goodness, his resistance to our evil. We, too, may know the burning heart, the experience of Cleopas and his friend on the way to Emmaus. We, too, may say with Paul, "It is no longer I who live, but Christ . . . lives in me." Quite apart from this personal experience of the living Lord, one may believe that the resurrection took place. For the objective evidence is impressive and may be convincing in itself. But full and joyful assurance can come only from within; only the Christ-filled heart can declare, "I know that my Redeemer lives!"

*There is a general impression today that the Bible has been discredited. Some people say that it is full of contradictions, others that it has been disproved by science, yet others that it has been superseded as a guide to life by more modern authorities. Are these criticisms valid? Or is the Bible still true? The word "true" can have so many different meanings that the Bible must be tested in a number of ways. How does it emerge from these tests?*

# 8

## Is the Bible True?

There are many people nowadays who think that the Bible has been discredited, or who at any rate no longer accept it as a sure guide for the journey of life. Some say that its pages have been disproved by science; others say that it is full of contradictions. Many question whether the stories recorded in it ever really happened—may they not be "cunningly devised fables"? It is usually the people who have never read the Bible who are absolutely certain about all this!

Now, the unbeliever is not greatly impressed when Christians fall back on the doctrine of the divine inspiration of Scripture and say, "The Bible is true throughout because God inspired it." True as this statement is, it cannot be of help to the man we have in mind; for if he believed it, he would no longer be an unbeliever! It is obviously arguing in a circle to say, "The Bible is true because the Bible is true." But is it not possible to meet the unbeliever on grounds that he can accept and with statements that he can verify? Can it be *demonstrated* that the Bible is reliable and accurate?

Now the question "Is it true?" may convey a number of quite different meanings. We therefore propose to illustrate six of these meanings and apply them as tests to the Bible. Because the Bible contains a number of different kinds of literature, such as history, moral instruction, poetry, and prophesy, not all six of these tests can be applied to every part of the Bible. But let us see how the Book emerges from the careful use of these tests.

1. Take the question, "Is it true that Julius Caesar landed in Britain in 55 b.c.?" In this connection the phrase means— did it actually happen; is it historically true? We inquire, then, first of all: Is the Bible historically true; did the events recorded in it actually happen? This can be tested in several ways, of which we will mention two.

First, there is the evidence from archeology or ancient remains. Jericho, for example, has been excavated, not only the city of Roman times, but the foundations of the more ancient city. The date and manner of its destruction have been scientifically computed and are found to confirm the biblical narrative in Joshua. Again, the discovery of the Moabite stone confirms and supplements the narrative of the Book of Kings, just as the fact that there actually was a seven-branched lampstand in the temple at Jerusalem is confirmed by the carving of this on the Arch of Titus, still standing in Rome.

Second, there is the evidence of contemporary written records. We have space for but one example. The invasion of Judea by the Assyrian King Sennacherib is described in 2 Kings, chapters 18 and 19, and in several oracles of the prophet Isaiah. But we have also the inscriptions of Sennacherib himself; and here we find the same events described, though naturally with a different interpretation and from a different point of view. These inscriptions, like the edicts of Cyrus the Persian or the writings of Josephus, confirm the biblical record that the events described did actually take place.

2. But the word "true" takes on quite a different meaning when we inquire, for example, "Is the philosophy of Karl Marx true?" In this sense "Is it true?" means, does it correspond with the facts, is it an accurate account of things, a true doctrine, a true interpretation of the world? Using the word in this sense, can we say that the biblical view of the world and of life, of God and of man, is a true interpretation? This can only be tested by correspondence with our actual experience of life itself. For example, the biblical doctrine of the fall and the radical sinfulness of man—does this correspond with the facts of history and of our present world situation? Or again, is history an arena, the scene of a constant struggle between the kingdom of God and the powers of evil, as the Bible teaches; or is it a gradual progress toward Utopia? It is evident that the biblical doctrines are confirmed by life, experience, and history; they correspond with the nature of things.

3. "Are the maxims of Confucius true?" Here we are thinking of true morality, a sure and safe guide to conduct. The truth we have in mind has reference to practical wisdom, the true way of life. Is the Bible then a guide to conduct? Does "the straight and narrow way" described and commanded therein lead on to life? Are the maxims of the Proverbs, the precepts of the Sermon on the Mount, and the ethical exhortations of the apostolic letters true in this sense? This claim can obviously be tested only in living—and it has been tested in all ages by myriads of human beings both negatively and positively, both by disobedience and obedience to "the Way." It has been proved beyond doubt that the Bible (or rather the Lord who speaks in and through its precepts) does create sound, strong, and attractive character. Such character, by the dynamic and positive quality of its

goodness, has ever been the salt of the earth and the light of the world. It has been abundantly demonstrated that "Every one . . . who hears these words of mine [the ethical and moral precepts of the Sermon on the Mount] and does them will be like a wise man who built his house upon the rock" (Matthew 7:24).

4. "Are the plays of Shakespeare true?" Here we are thinking of the extent to which his writings present a true mirror of life. A book in this sense may be true character study, reliable autobiography, or biography. Is the Bible in its portrayal of many and varied characters true to life? Now, anyone who has read the Bible must have been impressed by the realism of its characters; there is no attempt made to idealize man. Some of the stories are hardly suitable for reading at a drawing-room tea party! Not only the heroism and generosity of David, for example, are given to us, but also his lust and cruelty. These are real men and women, and that is one reason why the Bible stories remain so gripping: They show us life.

Noting here that a story may be true to life without being historically true may be helpful. When Jesus created some of his parables, he was not necessarily suggesting that the incidents actually happened. They were typical, however, of what could happen in real life. Not all the Bible claims to be history, but it is all true; and as a preliminary to Bible study it is a necessary safeguard, therefore, to inquire in what sense a story is true.

5. When we ask the question, "Is it true that the discovery and use of atomic power will end the world?" we want to know whether or not the prediction will be fulfilled. In a similar fashion, we ask about the Bible whether or not it is a true prediction, a true unfolding of the future. Many parts of the Bible, such as the books of the prophets or the Revelation, do foretell. Amos foretold the downfall of Israel before

Assyria; Jeremiah, the capture of Jerusalem by the Babylonians; Isaiah, the advent of the Messiah. Did these events (and many others like them) come to pass? In each case the answer is "Yes." Should not this fact suggest to us that the remainder of the (as yet) unfulfilled predictions are likewise true?

6. "Is it true that a certain man is a hero?" The truth about a person is the disclosure or revelation of his inner nature or character. The Bible above all else claims to be the revelation of the mind, will, character, and nature of God. God who is personal has revealed himself in a Person, the Lord Jesus Christ. He is the truth. The full truth about a person cannot, however, be known apart from relationship with that person. When a man allows himself to be confronted by the living Word, Jesus Christ, he begins to know by direct awareness that he is in touch with "that which is" (Plato's phrase), the final and ultimate reality, the truth, the living God.

The Bible emerges from all these tests triumphantly. The truth does not need to be vindicated by elaborate argument. The answer to all these questions will become plain—if a man will first read the Bible!

*We all like to be able to reason things out. But non-Christians often complain of the tendency of Christians to evade difficulties by hiding behind the claim that the Bible is God's Word, a divine revelation. Does our reason permit us to accept such a revelation? What difference is there between faith and mere credulity; or is faith "believing what you know isn't true"?*

# 9

## Is Divine Revelation Contrary to Reason?

In a school examination on Scripture, a boy is said to have defined faith as "believing what you know isn't true"! It seems that many people have this same general idea in the back of their minds. They tend to regard revelation as contrary to reason, and to look upon saints as simpletons. On this view the man who is religious has made himself believe that which otherwise he would regard as irrational. It may then be helpful if we attempt to define the true relationship between reason and revelation, between that which men may discover through inquiry and that which God has disclosed chiefly in the Bible.

A short story from the newspaper will help to illustrate some of the main points of comparison and contrast. The police arrested a man who was suspected of being guilty of murder. By long and patient research they had discovered certain facts which pointed to his complicity in the crime. There had been footprints in the garden soil, an abandoned weapon, a little piece of torn clothing, and several other small clues. All this evidence, however, was not sufficient to fasten the crime upon him; whereupon the police had subjected the suspect to a long and searching cross-examination. At the end of several hours the man had broken down and made a confession. He then proceeded to *reveal* to the police certain facts which they had not *discovered*—and never could have discovered by their own inquiries and investigations.

This story has obvious limitations when applied to God, but if this is borne in mind, it can shed light on our subject.

In the first place it illustrates the contrast between something *achieved* and something *given*. The police discover by their own efforts certain clues; these discoveries are their own achievement. But it is the prisoner himself who reveals the full story, and this revelation is given to the police—they receive it. Now, man likewise can achieve much in the realm of knowledge by his own efforts. One need only mention Plato the philosopher, Columbus the explorer, Newton the scientist, to select three names from many, to make this evident. These giants of reason discovered many of the "clues" which help us to understand life and the world. And God intends man to discover as much as can be discovered in the sphere of knowledge. But there are severe limitations to human discovery through inquiry. In this connection we may cite the ancient question from the Book of Job, "Canst thou by searching find out God?" If the police in our story could only know the prisoner's mind and heart through revelation, is it likely that we can ever know God in any other way?

There is also the contrast between activity on one side and activity on both sides in the apprehension of truth. In using their reason in the process of inquiry and discovery, the police only were active. But when the prisoner made a confession, there was an activity of disclosure, or revelation, on his side. Now, a philosopher like Plato is searching for the truth, and the findings are the result of Plato's own activity. But this is not the case with the great figures of the Bible. For example, "The word of the Lord came to Jeremiah"; he was actually reluctant to be a prophet, and on occasions would have preferred to be silent: "If I say, 'I will not mention him, or speak any more in his name,' there is in my heart as it were a burning fire shut up in my bones, and I am weary with holding it in, and I cannot." (Jeremiah 20:9). The prophet felt the constraint of a *divine activity*. "I have put my words in your mouth"—the truth the prophet was to utter was revelation. Here we are dealing not with man's discovery, but with God's disclosure.

We may refer here to the misleading view of some liberal scholars who speak of the Bible as the record of man's search for God. The Hebrews, we are told, had a genius for religion, just as the Greeks had a flair for beauty or philosophy. But a study of Israel's history rather suggests that the Hebrews as a whole had a genius for false religion! The Bible is the record of God's self-revelation, not of man's discovery; of God's grace, not of man's achievement. "Men moved [Greek, 'carried along'] by the Holy Spirit spoke from God" (2 Peter 1:21). We do not mean to suggest that there is no activity on the human side in revelation. The police in our story asked for the truth and listened while it was disclosed. They also urgently desired to know. So also it is the man who prays to God, who waits upon God, who listens to God, whose desire is toward God—who *receives* the revelation. In revelation man's activity (and there is, as we have said, a human activity) is always a response to a prior divine activity. God reveals, and man receives the revelation.

Finally, there is the contrast between a knowledge of something and a knowledge of somebody. The knowledge of reality acquired by reason is impersonal. It is a knowledge about things or a knowledge *about* (not *of*) persons. It is, of course, possible to acquire a knowledge about God through reason. But theology in the Christian sense is the truth about God as revealed in his Word; and the word "revelation" belongs to the sphere of personal relationships. For example, one can only know a human friend (as distinct from knowing about him) if the friend chooses to make himself known. Knowledge of a person is always a gift of the person concerned. The knowledge of God is always the gift of God, and we can only know God because he has graciously willed to reveal himself.

Now, God has willed to reveal himself in many ways. He is revealed in the open book of nature around us: "Ever since the creation of the world his invisible nature, namely, his eternal power and deity, has been clearly perceived in the things that have been made" (Romans 1:20). He is revealed in the stirring events of human history. He revealed himself "by divers portions and in divers manners," under many aspects and in many ways, to men of old. But in all these ways that which God reveals is *himself*. He does not disclose *something,* or some body of impersonal knowledge, but himself, the living God as Creator and Redeemer. His full and final revelation is a Person, Jesus Christ.

We stress this fact because of the prevalence of the idea that reason leads us to one "set of truths" and revelation to another. Revelation is not a "set of truths"; that which is revealed is the living God in Jesus Christ. So, then, reason leads to impersonal knowledge (both useful and necessary); revelation to that personal knowledge of "the only true God" which is eternal life (John 17:3).

Our conclusion is therefore that reason and revelation are not contradictories but complementaries. They are both valuable and both essential. By the use of reason we may discover many things about the world and about life, discoveries which if rightly used may be beneficial to mankind. Furthermore, by reason we may discover some things about God. Many truths about God are evident even to the un-aided human reason: that God is, that he is one, that he is infinite and eternal—all this was known through the light of reason.

But reason can take us only a limited way. It cannot bring to us the knowledge we most desperately need, the knowledge *of* God, of his innermost heart, mind, and pur-pose; the true knowledge of man, his nature, and destiny; of the way of deliverance and life. Would reason ever have told us that God would become man, that he would bear the burden of our sin, that he would come to dwell within us? Would reason ever have disclosed to us that light of the knowledge of God which shone radiantly in the face of Jesus Christ? We may well thank God for our reason, our crown of glory and honor. But far more do we thank him for his revelation in Jesus Christ, the Sun of Righteousness and the Light of the World.

*We can, of course, understand Christians being interested in the New Testament, a book about Christ and his church. But why continue to use the Old Testament, which is a collection of books all about the Jews and their history? In addition, there are those who protest that the Old Testament conception of God is crude, that its morals are sub-Christian, and that the coming of Christianity has rendered it all obsolete. Is there any reason, therefore, why we should go on using it?*

# 10

## Why Continue to Use the Old Testament?

Although Christians naturally think highly of the New Testament, the book which contains the revelation of Jesus Christ, some people wonder why the Old Testament should also continue to be used. These numerous critics of the Old Testament complain that it is difficult and obscure, that its conception of God is crude and sub-Christian, that its morals are imperfect and even at times positively repulsive. In any case, they object, the Old Testament has been rendered obsolete if Christianity is the fulfillment. Would it not therefore be better to discard it and to concentrate on the New Testament? This was actually done by Marcion, a heretic of the second century, and his numerous followers. Might the church not have done better to have followed his lead?

We propose in this chapter to give some of the main reasons not only for the continued use of the Old Testament, but also for the traditional Christian conviction that it is part of the divine revelation.

To begin with an obvious point, it would clearly be quite

impossible to understand the New Testament apart from the Old. Could one understand a full-grown oak tree by refusing to study any of the earlier stages of its growth? The New Testament literature is the climax and fulfillment of that long period of historical development recorded in the Old Testament. Much of the New is intelligible only if one has read the Old. What, for example, would we make of the Letter to the Hebrews if we had never read the book of Leviticus? What meaning would be conveyed by such New Testament expressions as "the Messiah," "the covenant," "redemption," "the law and the prophets" (to select just a few) to a person unacquainted with the Old Testament? And what could be made of the frequent references in the New Testament to Old Testament characters, men like Abraham, Moses, David, Elijah, and Job? The quotations from the Old Testament—and they are very many—would likewise lose their meaning. This point need not be elaborated: The first serious consequence of neglecting the Old Testament is to make much of the New unintelligible.

Further, if one accepts the authority of the New Testament, this must include an acceptance of its teaching about the Old. Now it is uniformly claimed in the New Testament that the Old is also the Word of God, divine revelation. It is not the full and final revelation, but it is revelation: "In many and various ways God spoke of old to our fathers by the prophets" (Hebrews 1:1). The men of the Old Covenant were "moved by the Holy Spirit" and could preface their utterances by the formula "Thus says the Lord." According to the New Testament, the Old Testament is not a record of man's striving up after God, but the record of God's self-disclosure to man. God was active in the Old Covenant, and he is revealed in the Old Testament. It is the Word of God.

This leads up to what has always been the chief objection against the continued use of the Old Testament, an objection which has never been more clearly expressed than by the heretic Marcion. According to him, the God of the Old Testament is not the God of the New. The former is the stern God of justice, the latter the gracious God of love. Now since the former idea of God is untrue, or at least crude and imperfect, why not discard it, as well as the literature which contains it?

Now this contrast (ancient and modern) between the God of justice and the God of love, between the law and grace, wrath and mercy, is completely false and misleading. Justice and love, anger and compassion, are certainly not opposites. A love which was not just and did not react with indignation against evil would not be the holy *agape* seen in Jesus Christ, but sentimentality. People today tend to make this false contrast because they have a sentimental conception of "love." But anger and compassion are both manifestations of real love. The God of the Bible is both "a righteous God and Savior" (Isaiah 45:21).

Thus the God of the Old Testament is the God of love, "a God merciful and gracious, slow to anger, and abounding in steadfast love and faithfulness, keeping steadfast love for thousands, forgiving iniquity and transgression and sin" (Exodus 34:6-7). This revelation of God's nature ("the name of the Lord," v. 5) as love was given to Moses on Mount Sinai. So also the God of the New Testament is the God of justice and retribution. If Moses quaked with awe at Mount Sinai, then we who are come to Mount Zion are to be filled with yet greater reverence, serving God "with reverence and awe; for our God is a consuming fire" (Hebrews 12:21-22, 28-29). The alleged contrast between the Testaments simply does not exist. In *all* the Bible we "note . . . the kindness and the severity of God" (Romans 11:22).

Marcion himself soon discovered this. No sooner had he discarded the Old Testament than he had to start cutting sections out of the New. He found the just God of the law there also—for his particular theory it was most awkward!

The assertion that the morals of the Old Testament are imperfect and sometimes repulsive to modern man, the perpetrator of Belsen and Hiroshima, is almost humorous. If the claim is made seriously, it can only be due either to abysmal ignorance or to conceit. The presumption of such a claim will be obvious to anyone who will test himself against the highest moral standards of the Old Testament. Read the Ten Commandments (Exodus 20) or Psalm 24:3-5, or, best of all, Job's description of a good man (chapter 31), and then ask yourself if *you* have ever lived up to that. "What does the Lord require of you, but to do justice, and to love kindness, and to walk humbly with your God?" (Micah 6:8). "Thus says the Lord of hosts, Render true judgments, show kindness and mercy each to his brother, do not oppose the widow, the fatherless, the sojourner, or the poor; and let none of you devise evil against his brother in your heart" (Zechariah 7: 9-10). Crude and imperfect? We have never come within a mile of these moral standards!

Of course, there are morally shocking things in the Old Testament (as in the New). Just because it is a book about real men and women, it is therefore a mirror of human sin. There *are* great sinners and great sins in the Bible, just as there are great saints and great virtues. But no one objects to Shakespeare's *Othello* on the ground that Iago is a thoroughly evil and repulsive character. Most of the great characters of the Old Testament, however, are attractive, inspiring, stalwart, and great. Even though the Old Testament does not claim that men like Abraham, Joseph, Moses, Elijah, Jeremiah, and others are without sin, they are glorious examples of human character and personality at its best. One doubts if those who pretend to disparage Old Testament morals would care to be compared with them!

There remains one argument which is deserving of greater respect. Perhaps it can be expressed best in Paul's words. "When the perfect comes, the imperfect will pass away." Granted that the Old Testament *was* a partial revelation of God, is it not now superseded in the perfect, the New Testament revelation in Jesus Christ? Our Lord himself answers this question thus: "Think not that I have come to abolish . . . but to fulfill" (Matthew 5:17). Christ brings the Old Testament to completion; he gives to it its full meaning and content. Destroy it? Supersede it? On the contrary, he fills it up. We now see more clearly what it was all about, and for the first time its *full* meaning is disclosed. Previously "when they read the old covenant," the veil remained unlifted; "only through Christ is it taken away" (2 Corinthians 3:14). Christ is the content of the Old Testament. "You search the [Old Testament] scriptures . . . it is they that bear witness to me" (John 5:39). We therefore read the Old Testament for the *same* reason that we read the New—to come to Christ. The Old Testament is testimony to him: "Moses wrote of me." The risen Lord on the way to Emmaus "beginning with Moses and with all the prophets . . . interpreted to them in all the scriptures the things concerning himself" (Luke 24:27). Philip only did what all the apostles were doing when "beginning with this scripture" (the Old Testament at Isaiah 53) "he told him the good news of Jesus" (Acts 8: 35). The Old Testament is about Jesus. Ultimately, that is why we read it.

The people who read the Old Testament are never likely to ask, "Why continue to use it?" It is usually those who don't read it who ask the question! To know its pages is to love them. Regular and devoted readers have come to love the history, the laws, the songs, the oracles, the great characters, the immortal stories. They have found that he who is revealed in the New Testament lies hidden in the Old, and they delight to find him there. Why continue to read the Old Testament? Perhaps the only really convincing answer is the ancient one, "Come and see."

*The suggestion is sometimes made that the elaborate teaching of the epistles in the New Testament was added to Christianity, an invention of the apostles. Our Lord's message seemed to be so simple and homely, and we do not find him using such difficult theological terms as "propitiation" and "atonement." Is there then a contrast between Jesus and Paul? And would it not be better for us to return to the simplicities of the Gospels?*

# 11

## Did the Apostles Complicate
## the Simple Message of Jesus?

At the present time there is a marked tendency among some people to contrast the simple story of the life and teaching of Jesus as recorded in the Gospels with what they consider to be the more complicated doctrines of the apostles. What a world of difference there is, we are told, between the Gospel of Mark with its interesting and graphic stories, and the elaborate arguments of the Epistle to the Romans. What a striking contrast between the simple ethical teaching of the Sermon on the Mount and the abstruse theology of the Letter to the Hebrews! Again, compare the homely language used by Jesus with the technical and theological words —such as "propitiation," "justification," and "ransom"— found in the letters of the apostles. Should we not return to the simplicities of the Gospels, endeavoring to rediscover the Jesus of history?

This vague general attitude is only too well known. On closer examination it is found to crystallize into three main objections. The first concerns the person of Jesus Christ.

In the simple Gospels it appears that Jesus was concerned not so much with his own person as with teaching the good news of the kingdom of God. The apostles, however, have made the person of Christ central and have "worked up" a dogma of his divinity.

The next objection has reference to the work of Jesus. In the Gospels, so it is said, the universal Father accepts all who turn to him, and nothing more is required. No bleeding sacrifice is needed to reconcile the returning prodigal to the loving father in Luke 15. But the apostles expound difficult theories of atonement, making the death of Christ and the shedding of his blood essential to the acceptance by God of the sinner. In the third objection, we are told that Jesus taught that good works alone make a man acceptable to God (Matthew 7:21; 12:37, 50; 25:14-46). Paul, on the other hand, teaches the elaborate and less natural theory of justification by faith.

We propose now to answer these three objections in turn. And they will be answered, not by appealing to the letters of the apostles, but to those very sources which the objector is said to accept, the so-called "simple" Gospels. Before doing so, however, it is not irrelevant to ask the question, "Who gave us the Gospels in which this simple teaching is recorded?" Has the objector realized that the letters of the apostles were in circulation before the Gospels? Does he appreciate that the Gospels were written by the apostles? Mark and Luke are no exceptions to this, since the former records the teaching of the apostle Peter and the latter was the traveling companion of Paul and received his material from the original (apostolic) eyewitnesses (Luke 1:1-4).

The Gospels are apostolic. It is therefore a patent fallacy to contrast them with the epistles. Both alike are apostolic testimony, and it is hardly likely that the apostles would contradict themselves. Furthermore, since many of the epistles were written before the Gospels, the apostles must have simplified and not complicated their message. This is the exact reverse of the popular objection—and it is equally untrue. The apostles neither complicate nor simplify; it is the same message in both epistles and Gospels, as we now propose to show in answering the three objections.

The person of Jesus Christ is central in the Gospels as in the epistles. Not only is he the center of the story, but he is also the center of his own teaching. He teaches in his own name with absolute authority, replacing the "Thus says the Lord" of the prophet with "I say unto you." For his words he claims unique importance (Matthew 7:24-27; Mark 13:31). His word alone is the authority to interpret and fulfill the Mosaic Law, itself a divine institution (Matthew 5). Not only is he above the law, but he is also Lord of the sabbath (Matthew 12:1-13), of the temple (Matthew 12:6), and of every other holy institution. He is greater than Moses (Matthew 5:21-22), wiser than Solomon, and a greater prophet than Jonah (Matthew 12:39-42). The outstanding Hebrew king David calls him Lord (Matthew 22:41-46). The prophets are the servants: he is the "beloved Son" (Luke 20:9-18).

He is the creator of the new Israel (Matthew 16:13-20) and establishes a new covenant in his own blood (Mark 14:24). He is the destined judge of the whole human race (Matthew 7:21-23; 13:30, 41; 25:11-13, etc.). Men are invited to come to him and find rest (Matthew 11:28), to believe on him (John 7:38), to follow him (Matthew 4:19). Prayer is to be offered in his name (John 14:13), and men are to confess him openly (Matthew 10:32).

His character is unique and perfect; his mighty deeds without precedent. He is the unique Son to whom the Father speaks in his baptism and at his transfiguration, and to whom all things have been delivered. His knowledge of the Father is unique; he is the sole Mediator between God and man (Matthew 11:27). These many references are all taken from the synoptic Gospels, and John summarizes the whole testimony of Jesus concerning himself when he says, "I and the Father are one," "He who has seen me has seen the Father." Do the apostles say more than this?

The work of Jesus Christ is, of course, intimately related to his person. Once he had established the truth regarding the latter (Matthew 16:16), he was in a position to speak more plainly about his vocation as Savior (v. 21). And quite clearly the Gospels attach decisive importance to the death of Jesus. The three greatest crises of his ministry— the baptism, the transfiguration, Gethsemane—all have reference to his work as suffering Messiah and Redeemer. The whole story moves forward to the climax of the cross, which is not merely the end, but the fulfillment of the ministry. Jesus declared, "for this purpose I have come to this hour" (John 12:27).

Why does Mark devote six out of a total of sixteen chapters, and John eight out of twenty-one chapters, to the story of the passion, death, and resurrection of Christ? Why this disproportion? The reason is that "the Son of man came not to be served, but to serve, and to give his life as a ransom for many." In this saying of Jesus we find the very word to which objection is made by some in the writings of Paul.

Jesus taught that the kingdom, present in his person, could only be established through his death. Through his sacrifice alone could the union, the reconciliation of man to God, be achieved. He said, "This is my blood of the covenant, which is poured out for many" (Mark 14:24). If we are to take the teaching of Jesus seriously, how can this part of it be ignored? Can anyone seriously claim to be living out the ethical teaching of the Sermon on the Mount (e.g.,

"Blessed are the pure in heart") apart from the power of Calvary?

Justification by faith is proclaimed in almost every chapter of the Gospels. The outstanding feature of the ministry of Jesus was his friendship with sinners. Even his enemies realized this when they described him as "a friend of tax collectors and sinners!" Unlike the Pharisees, Jesus did not associate with men on the ground of their merits, but on the ground of his own gracious love. He did not wait for their good works to qualify them for fellowship with himself, but he went forth to seek and save them as they were. The stories of Zacchaeus and the penitent woman in the house of Simon the Pharisee are but typical of his whole ministry. "Your sins are forgiven . . . your faith has saved you" (Luke 7:48, 50); God's grace in Christ, and not human merit, was the ground of acceptance.

Jesus contrasted the Pharisee who sought to justify himself by an accurate recital of his good works, with the publican who cast himself on God's mercy; "This man [the publican] went down to his house justified [the very Pauline word to which some object!] rather than the other." This vital faith must, of course, issue in good works: that is the test of its reality. The final standard of judgment is faith, but real faith, "faith working through love" (Galatians 5:6).

In all these respects it will be seen that the apostles are simply expounding what is already implicit in the life and teaching of Jesus. Indeed, that is an understatement, for most of what the apostles write is quite explicit in the Gospels. At no point do they add anything new. It is true, of course, that the Holy Spirit, working through the apostles, does bring out and interpret what Jesus had said and done. During his early ministry many things had not been fully understood, and some things he had been unable to say. "I have yet many things to say to you, but you cannot bear them now." The letters of the apostles are the fulfillment of the accompanying promise: "When the Spirit of Truth comes, he will guide you into all the truth . . . for he will take what is mine and declare it to you" (John 16:13-14).

*Unbelief is fashionable today. There is a widespread idea that it is "scientific" to doubt the Bible and a tendency to embrace the latest theory just because it is the latest. But is this the true scientific attitude? Why is it, for example, that so many outstanding scientists have been convinced Christians? Does the scientific knowledge of our own century stand in opposition to Christian belief, or are science and religion two different aspects of the same quest for truth?*

# 12

## Has Science Disproved Religion?

This is the age of science, and the notion that science has discredited religion is widespread. Religion, many say, may have served a useful function in the "prescientific era," but the progress of science has shown one religious belief after another to be untenable, and soon there will be none left. It is only a matter of time! True, this attitude was to some extent characteristic of science in the nineteenth century, or rather of the materialistic interpretation (i.e., misinterpretation) of scientific facts. But there is much in the science of this century which favors the Christian view of the world. Unfortunately these facts are not yet widely known.

The purpose of this chapter is to show that there need never be any conflict between true science and true religion. That there has been such a conflict is not denied, but this conflict was, or is, largely due to misunderstanding. The misunderstanding was not all on the side of the scientists by any means. The church has often been ignorant, superstitious, and dogmatic, fanatically and fearfully opposing new truth. It was the church, for instance, which opposed Copernicus and his new conception of the solar system, now universally accepted. Science as well as religion has had its martyrs. That is why it is so necessary that the true nature and function of both should be understood. In this way needless conflict might be avoided and give way to fruitful cooperation. We shall attempt then to describe the true sphere and nature of each.

First, science and religion represent quite different aspects of man's quest for reality. To express this graphically, science fishes in the sea of truth with one kind of net, religion with another. There are many kinds of "fish" which cannot be caught by the net of science; there are aspects of reality or existence of which science can have no knowledge. Science is a *quantitative* approach to reality; that is, it deals only with those aspects of reality which are capable of measurement in some way. That is why the basic science is mathematics. But a very large aspect of reality just cannot be measured thus; it slips through this particular sort of net.

The beauty of a sunset or a symphony, the heroism of the patriot, the love of a mother, and the goodness of a saint—such realities fall outside this kind of approach. The patent fallacy of the materialist is to conclude that they therefore do not exist. The true conclusion is that the scientific method deals with one abstracted aspect of reality. It is a valid and valuable approach, but it is only one; religion is another. Religion is the personal approach to reality. These approaches are complementary, not contradictory. A scientist may discover a great deal about his wife by the scientific method, e.g., her exact weight and chemical constitution! But he can only *know* his wife through personal relationship, trust, and love. The one kind of knowledge cannot lead to the other, however much it is extended. They are different in kind, and both are necessary.

Second, science describes, whereas religion interprets. This second distinction is of fundamental importance. We may express this in another way by saying that science asks the question "What?" and religion asks the question "Why?" Science is concerned with the accurate description of processes (what happens), whereas religion is concerned with value and meaning. An illustration may make this clearer. Let the reader ask the question, "How did I come into existence?" One aspect of the answer would be to attempt to describe the process in terms of the science of biology, and thus to trace the development of the organism from the single cell at the moment of conception up to its present complexity. All such information is concerned with what actually happened. But suppose we ask the other question, "Why?" What is behind these processes science describes, and what is their meaning and significance? Religion answers, "God created you" (see Psalm 139:13-16). Now, these two accounts are not in any way contradictory. A description of process (science) cannot contradict a statement of ultimate origin and meaning (philosophy and religion).

This is a fundamental principle which should be applied in all instances where science and religion are said to contradict. In this connection it is important to draw attention to the misleading word "explains." Science is often said to explain this, that, and the other. But, strictly speaking, science explains nothing. For to explain a thing is to account for it in terms of its origin and significance. Here, then, is a fruitful source of confusion due to the misuse of words. We are often told, for example, that science *explains* a thunderstorm in terms of electrical phenomena. But that is how science *describes* a thunderstorm; the explanation goes far deeper.

Third, the distinction between science and religion is the distinction between human inquiry and divine revelation.

Now, to begin with the latter, that which God reveals is himself. He discloses *himself* to man as the Living God, Creator, Lord, and Redeemer. The Bible is the textbook of this revelation. Science is concerned with information about the world, and God intends man to find this out by careful, disinterested, and patient inquiry. We can attempt to state this distinction in a sentence. The Bible is concerned with the revelation of God, science with information about the world.

The Bible is not primarily concerned with information about the world; i.e., its purpose is not to teach us cosmology, physics, geology, or biology. On the other hand, science is not concerned with God, and the scientist as such can have no knowledge of him. For the living God cannot be enclosed in the net of a quantitative approach to reality! He can only be known in personal relationship: not in the relationship "I-it" (science), but "I-Thou" (religion). Thus the Bible and the scientific textbook have quite different purposes. Why, therefore, confuse them? As a great scientist who was also a Christian said, "The purpose of the Holy Spirit is to teach us how we can reach heaven, and not how the heavens are moved." Galileo also said, "The aim of the Holy Spirit in the Holy Scriptures is much higher than that of teaching us the wisdom of this world."

Why science and religion are sometimes found to be in opposition may now be clear. On the one hand, the scientist may fail to recognize the severe limitations of his own particular method and assume that he is dealing with the whole of reality. Fortunately, this mistake is hardly ever made nowadays, and modern scientists are often the first to own that their knowledge is partial and abstract. The scientist may, however, leave behind his own limited sphere and presume to make theological or religious statements. He has, of course, not the slightest authority for doing this. The fact that a man is an excellent farmer does not lend any authority to his pronouncements on, say, ancient history. But, on the other hand, the man of God may also leave his proper sphere and presume to make scientific pronouncements. Again, he has not the slightest authority for doing this.

This does not imply, however, that scientific knowledge and divine revelation are in two separate watertight compartments with no relationship between them at all. There are distinct spheres, and grasping the distinction is vital, but realities which are distinct need not be kept in isolation. After all, they are concerned with the same universe, even if from different aspects. Furthermore, the scientist may be a Christian believer and the believer a scientist. Many great scientists have been outstanding Christians. It is also a fact (which could be demonstrated from history) that a knowledge of the living God tends to create a keen desire for information about his world. On the other hand, we may always hope that they who study "the mysterious universe" will be led to him whose "everlasting power and divinity" it declares. There should therefore be fruitful interchange and cooperation.

But when all this has been said, the fact still remains that they are distinct spheres. The way to knowledge about the world will always (in this life) be the way of dispassionate and careful inquiry. Science itself is part of the divine intention for us, and God will not disclose to us that which we ought to find out for ourselves. There is, however, that which we could never have found out for ourselves. "Can you find out the deep things of God?" Happily God has fully revealed himself to us through his living Word, the Lord Jesus Christ, in the holy Scriptures. This knowledge can only be reached in one way, whether by philosopher or peasant, scientist or saint—the way of personal trust and obedience.

*Christianity is not the only great religion in the world. There are millions of people who are devout followers of Confucius, Buddha, and Mohammed, to mention only three other faiths. If these people are sincere, are they not all traveling the same way, different paths to the one destination? While admitting that Christianity is one of the great religions, some people find it far too exclusive, and prefer to believe that there are others worshiping the same God under different forms.*

# 13

## Are the Other Religions Also Ways to God?

In the New Testament, Christianity is sometimes referred to as "the Way." Is not this, however, an arrogant claim; and should it not rather be called "a way"? For while Jesus Christ is certainly a way to God, perhaps even the best and highest way, surely he is not the only way? Others claim that there are several other excellent ways to God, such as the lofty monotheism of Zoroaster of Persia, the way of renunciation of the Buddha, the way of mysticism in Neo-Platonism, and so on.

Confronted by this variety of ways to God, the ordinary man is apt to adopt one of two attitudes. "They are obviously *all wrong,* since they contradict one another, and the whole of religion is humbug." Or he may say, "They are *all right,* for they are all saying the same thing in many different ways. Each one is a color, and all together make the rainbow. There are twelve gates into the Eternal City, and you may enter through Confucius, Plato, Mohammed, Moses, Buddha, or Jesus—just as you prefer."

Whatever view *we* may adopt, the teaching of the Bible on this matter is quite clear. The general attitude of the Old Testament to other religions is well expressed in the phrase "the gods of the nations are idols." Our Lord was quite explicit, "I am the true and living way [this is probably the correct way to translate John 14:6], no one comes to the Father but by me" (compare Matthew 11:27). There is also the statement of Peter, "And there is salvation in no one else [than Jesus], for there is no other name . . . by which we must be saved" (Acts 4:12). The fact cannot be escaped that unlike many other religions (e.g., Hinduism) Christianity is exclusive and intolerant. The early Christians refused to allow the image of Christ to be placed in the Pantheon alongside the other "gods"—the latter were like Dagon before the ark (1 Samuel 5:3).

However, to infer from this that the attitude of the Bible to all other religions is simply negative and destructive would be a mistake. To say that they are not ways to God, not means of salvation, is one thing; to say that there is no truth or good at all in any of them is another. The former statement is true, the latter untrue. The Lord Jesus says both "No" and "Yes" to the great world religions. We will take the "Yes" first.

Jesus affirms and fulfills any truth or good which may be found in the other religions, and such positive elements are to be found. They are, for example, a striking testimony to man's agelong hunger and search for God. If other races and ages had not sought after God, we might well doubt the truth that man was made for him. Paul reminded the pagans at Athens that all men had been created "that they should seek God, in the hope that they might feel after him, and find him" (Acts 17:27). In many ways men are genuinely and sincerely *seeking* for God, and we fully acknowledge the devotion of many in the great world religions. But hunger is not bread. It is the true Bread of Life which satisfies this hunger.

Then too, the other great religions are a testimony to the eternal moral law of God. How significant it is that almost all the great religions have the golden rule in one form or another; they include in a negative and sometimes distorted form that which Jesus gives in a positive and perfect form (Matthew 7:12). They each obtained it for themselves; it was not copied or borrowed. What does this fact indicate? There must be an eternal moral law written in our very nature (Romans 2:14-15). The other religions, or ethical systems, *may* therefore possess a true, howbeit partial and usually distorted, knowledge of goodness. The courage of the Stoic, the courtesy of the Confucian, the kindness of the Buddhist—these are real virtues and real values. Of that moral law Christ is the fulfillment.

So also the world religions do contain many elements of truth, even if partial and mixed with error. The pyramids of Egypt do testify to the truth of immortality. The blood-baths of the mystery religions do bear witness at least to man's conscious need of redemption "through blood." And it cannot be without significance that the Greek and Stoic philosophers knew that the world was created and sustained by the Logos (the Word of God). In these and many other ways other religions have had intuitions of the truth. But Jesus Christ is God's "Yes" to their hunger for the living God, to their quest for goodness, and to their search for truth.

All this, however, must not blind us to the fact that in Christ God says a final and decisive "No" to these other "ways." They are essentially mistaken, and even corrupt. What is meant here may be made clear by an Old Testament story. Human beings once in their history decided to build a gigantic tower up which they could climb into heaven

(Genesis 11). We smile at their folly? But that is precisely what the great world religions try to do; they are man's attempt to *ascend* to God. That is why the illustration of the ladder is often used in them: There is the ladder of good works, the ladder of contemplation, the ladder of knowledge, the ladder of renunciation, up which one may climb to ——? But the "heaven is high above the earth," that is to say, the Holy God is far removed from sinful man. All human attempts to bridge that gulf are pathetic and futile towers of Babel built up into empty space and leading—nowhere. Babel, alas, is worse than futile; it is a monument of human pride. How arrogant of sinful man to suppose that he can reach a level with God by his own efforts! Human folly and pride are seen at their worst in religion. Remember that it was Pharisee and scribe and priest who crucified the Son of God.

Thus religions are man's attempt to *ascend,* but Christianity is the good news of the God who *descends*—not Babel, but Bethlehem. The moral chasm between God and man cannot be crossed from man's side; it is God who descends and comes to us. The ladder of the patriarch's dream (Genesis 28:10-22) is the cross of Christ, as we learn from John 1:51. This is God's amazing good news: He has come right down to us on our level, for "he humbly stooped in his obedience even to die, and to die upon the cross" (Philippians 2:8, Moffatt).

Because this is true, then all the other ways are false. If God has come down to us, we do not need to keep on trying to ascend to him. For man's need is not to climb a little more strenuously up his self-constructed Babels, but to receive in adoring gratitude and utter trust the God who has come down to him. Christianity is the news of grace, and grace is love *coming down* alongside sinful man to meet his need.

All religions have this in common with Christianity: They all recognize that the goal or objective is union with God. They differ from Christianity in this respect: This union with God, they say, can be reached by the ascent of man to God's level. They differ greatly from one another in that they set forth different ways of making this ascent, but the common feature is there. Christianity is unique because it is the religion of descent, the story of the God "who for us men, and for our salvation, came down from heaven," the God of Bethlehem, Calvary, and Pentecost. Between the two—ascent and descent—there can be no compromise.

If we may misquote but apply the substance of Paul's words: "What fellowship has a religion of grace with a religion of merit? Or what is there in common between the way of the descending God and the ways of ascending man?" We have here not only the real distinction between Christianity and all other religions, but also the distinction between real biblical Christianity and its many perversions. Christianity is not only the way to God—it is primarily the way of God down to man. There is only one such way.

*Nobody can read the Bible without realizing that miracles play a considerable part in its story. Yet, in our own day we never seem to see the kind of miracles there described. Did these miracles really take place; or were pious recorders "writing up" contemporary events? In any case, is it possible for miracles to take place at all? Do they not violate the laws of nature?*

# 14

## Do Miracles Really Take Place?

There was a time when miracles were regarded as one of the most convincing proofs of the Christian faith. Nowadays many regard them as the greatest hindrance to its acceptance. Before stating the reasons for this change of attitude, it is perhaps worth noting that Christ himself did not expect miracles to produce faith. He always regarded a request for a "sign" as sinful and affirmed that even the greatest miracle, resurrection from the dead, would make no impression upon unbelievers (Luke 16:31). Although the statement needs some qualification, we may sum up the teaching of Jesus on this matter in some such words as these: "Miracles do not produce faith, but faith produces miracles." For it is faith which makes possible the working of God's power in a miraculous way; faith is the necessary condition, not the result of miracle. Therefore our purpose is not to attempt to prove that miracles happen, but rather to remove the hindrances to human confidence in divine power to effect what seems impossible to men (Mark 10:27).

Now, most of these hindrances today come, not from science, but from false theories or assumptions imposed upon (not derived from) the facts disclosed to science. It is vital to grasp this distinction—the distinction between facts and the interpretation (or misinterpretation) of them. For facts and for genuine scientific inquiry we do well to have great respect; for pseudoscience, for inadequate or misleading theories imposed upon the facts, we do well to have equally great disrespect. Four of these latter theories must be mentioned, because they are the fount and origin of unbelief in miracles. They are all the more dangerous because in the popular mind they are often unconscious assumptions.

The first is the fallacy of mechanism, the error of supposing that nature, the universe, is analogous to a machine. The analogy is clearly absurd, for whoever heard of a self-made, self-running, self-sufficient machine! As the physicists now assure us, not even the atom, much less a human being, "works" in this way. This error still haunts the popular mind in the form of deism. God made the world once and then left it to "run" by itself, just as the watchmaker, having made the watch, leaves it to go on working. But God is not outside the world; he is both within it and beyond it, "upholding all things by the word of his power." If he is within it, then his acts of power (miracles) are not alien intrusions from outside, but ordered operations from within.

Closely allied to that error is the fallacy of materialism, the assumption that material forces are the only forces in the universe. If they were, then admittedly miracles would be impossible. But this prejudice is contrary to our experience of life and the world, in which events are constantly happening through other than physical causes. If a man lifts a chair, he makes use of material forces, but the ground of his action is thought and will.

A third error is that of personifying "the Laws of Nature"

(with capital letters!) as if they were independent entities to which even God is subject. But what, after all, is a law of nature? It is simply an observed regularity, a statistical average, a general description of how things do behave, not how they must behave. It is curious how these two things— do behave, must behave—are usually confused. That things do behave in a regular and ordered way is itself a revelation of the divine nature, "For God is not a God of confusion" (1 Corinthians 14:33). But to infer from this that they *must* behave in that way is a logical fallacy. Mr. Smith, being a man of ordered habits, invariably catches the 8:15 A.M. train to the city, but he is not compelled to do so. Likewise the laws of nature are the habits of God. He determines them— they do not determine him. It is interesting to observe that this idea, so beloved of Victorian materialists, that all events are determined by final and immutable laws, has now been abandoned by physicists themselves. For example, we are told by them that the revolution of an electron around the nucleus of an atom cannot be predicted. This discloses something analogous to human freedom (the principle of indeterminacy).

The fourth fallacy is that of supposing a miracle to be a breach or violation of the laws of nature. This popular misconception of miracle cannot be true, for the God of grace is also the God of nature, and it is not conceivable that God should work against his own order. This, however, raises the question which brings us to the heart of our subject, the relation of miracle to natural law. A simple illustration may help to illuminate this.

A father is sitting in his armchair by the fire reading the newspaper. His little son has gone out into the garden to play in the snow. After a time the father hears a knock at the door, for the boy is very cold and wants to come in to the fire. In response to the child's need made known in the knocking, the father rises and opens the door, and admits the child. This is a typical and familiar event in the realm of human personal relationships; consider its significance. The door does not open of itself in response to the child's need. Had it done so we should rightly regard the event as a breach in the order and laws of the physical world. The father opens the door, but in so doing he acts within, and at no point does he break, those physical laws. But his action, while including, transcends them. In response to human need, and often in answer to human petition (which is prayer), the heavenly Father acts personally to meet that need. His action takes place, not in opposition to, but within and through the laws of the lower sphere—and yet transcends them. Indeed, we may aptly apply the words of Jesus about the Mosaic laws to the laws of nature: "I have not come to abolish [the law], but to fulfill them."

We have interesting analogies within our normal experience of the way in which the laws of one realm of being are included and yet transcended in a higher order. The laws of physics operate also in the science of chemistry, and both are included in the organic realm. Animal life again includes and yet transcends the organic; and still higher, human life, while including all the animal, far outspans it, introducing entirely new possibilities through the presence of mind. Each realm includes the lower, with its laws, which still operate, and yet are transcended. Why, then, should it be regarded as unreasonable to suppose that there is a yet higher realm than human life, including all the laws of our present life, and yet going far beyond them?

In Jesus Christ this higher order—not disorder—this "realm of God" is revealed, and its possibilities are disclosed in his mighty works. Are not the laws of health fulfilled, not broken, in the healing miracles of Jesus? Or as Augustine says, when he transformed the water into wine, or multiplied the loaves, was he not speeding up a miraculous transformation that he is constantly effecting in nature—" 'Twas springtide when he blest the bread, and harvest when he brake." As he never ceased to insist in parable after parable, the kingdom of God is like the kingdom of nature, analogous but higher.

If this is the case, why is it that to us miracle does appear as an intrusion? The reason is not far to seek. The real intruder in the world is sin. Sin is the lawbreaker, for "sin is lawlessness," and its fruits disorder and chaos. God intervenes to arrest the intruder and to restore the original health, wholeness, and harmony. An illustration will make this clear. A man is suffering from acute appendicitis, and if the processes of the disease are not arrested, he will die. And so the surgeon "intervenes" with the knife, and by his decisive and timely intrusion, the disease is arrested and health restored. But the surgeon's intrusion is itself not lawless; on the contrary, he is acting upon the highest laws of medical science.

The organism of humanity was afflicted with disease and sin, and but for the intrusion of the divine Physician, death would have been inevitable. In Jesus Christ the great intervention took place, by which the processes of sin and death were arrested, and health and salvation were bestowed. But the intervention itself is a revelation of the higher realm of law, the law of the divine nature which is love. The miracles of Jesus are revelations of divine love, "signs" of the presence of the kingdom of God.

But not only the miracles, for Jesus Christ himself is *the* miracle. He is the intervention of divine love, and all who receive him and experience his miraculous power and grace are able to join him in the confident prayer, "Abba, Father, all things are possible to thee" (Mark 14:36).

*This important question has always exercised the minds of men and women. Are our lives snuffed out at the end like a candle? Or is there anything in the various arguments for survival that have been propounded? Christians claim that the Bible reveals a good deal concerning the life beyond. What then is the Christian teaching about the afterlife?*

# 15

## What Happens After We Die?

"If a man die, shall he live again?" This question from the Book of Job is one that has always engaged the thoughts of men and women. The cynic might reply that the answer is anybody's guess, but the thoughtful ways in which people down the ages have sought to delve into this mystery cannot be so lightly dismissed. Before we state what Christians believe concerning life after death, we must look for a moment or two at some other arguments for survival which have been propounded.

There is first of all the sense that life here on earth is so unjust that it demands a sequel where wrongs will be righted and righteousness vindicated. Men feel with the psalmist: "I was envious at the foolish, when I saw the prosperity of the wicked. . . . Behold, these are the ungodly, who prosper in the world" (Psalm 73:3, 12, A.V.). Surely there is a future life where the balance of things is redressed? Again, there is a feeling of incompleteness about this life, so that a future world is needed in which to exercise the functions whose possibilities have never fully been realized here. Readers of Browning's poetry will be familiar with this kind of thought, the teleological argument, as it is sometimes called. From very many quotations which illustrate the point, we select from "Andrea del Sarto":

> Ah, but a man's reach should exceed his grasp,
> Or what's a Heaven for?

and from "A Grammarian's Funeral":

> . . . did not he throw on God,
>    (He loves the burthen)—
> God's task to make the heavenly period
>    Perfect the earthen?

Men and women made in the image of God are creatures of infinite value. We possess a moral sense and a capacity for knowing God. Is it conceivable that death (that is, physical death) can be the end and that God will thus lightly discard values that mean so much to him? There is yet a further argument—from desire. This derives from the fact that in the physical realm there is an answer to every hunger. Must not this be equally true of the spiritual realm? Or are our desires after immortality mere mockery? There has been implanted within our hearts a longing for, and an expectation of, life after death. God made us thus, and our longings and expectations must correspond with realities beyond.

The general arguments from experience are the easiest to understand and are perhaps the most convincing. In the depth of our being we believe in life after death—and always have done so! The men who lived millenniums ago were vastly different from ourselves in many respects, but we agree with them across the ages in this, because they buried their dead with great care and believed in survival. Archeologists have found these burial places most fruitful centers of discovery. And what is the evidence to be deduced from them? Dr. Langdon, for example, has said: "The theological view running through Babylonia before 2,000 B.C. was of a heaven for the righteous, whom the gods might receive into paradise, where is the bread and water of eternal life."

Such, very summarily stated, are some of the speculations of men supporting the view that there is a life beyond the grave. Now what has Christianity to say? The Christian readily admits that his knowledge of the life to come, though real, is limited; God has seen fit only partly to withdraw the veil. But, as we saw in an earlier chapter, the Christian faith rests upon the assured triumph of the raising of Jesus Christ from the dead, and its teaching therefore comes from One who has himself returned from the other side. Further, the Christian believer already possesses eternal life, in part although not in its fullness, and therefore knows what it is like essentially. The eternal world is not altogether a mystery; much has been revealed to us in the Bible through God's spokesmen and particularly through God's Son.

We know that there is an intermediate state into which all souls pass immediately after death and where they remain until the resurrection. Good and evil alike enter this abode of the dead, called in the Hebrew *sheol,* and in the Greek *hades.* The fact that *hades* is translated *hell* in the Authorized Version of our Bible warns us to be very careful in our use of this term. Hades is not the final state of the wicked. Our Lord himself, after his death upon the cross, descended into hades to preach the gospel to the departed (see 1 Peter 3:19; 4:6); the Apostles' Creed contains the statement "He descended into *hell."* (See also Acts 2:31.)

Although all souls pass into this intermediate state, yet "there is a great gulf fixed" (Luke 16:26) between the "saved" and the "lost." The saved are said to be in *paradise,* a beautiful Persian word denoting a park which the Hebrew people took over into their own language. It describes a state of peace and happiness, and we recall our Lord's words to the thief on the cross, "Today you will be with me in Paradise" (Luke 23:43). The intermediate state is a conscious state: In Revelation 6:9-11, we see the departed and disembodied spirits in a state of consciousness calling upon God; in John 11:26 Jesus says to Martha, as she mourns the loss of Lazarus, "Whoever lives and believes in me shall never die." In Philippians 1:23 Paul says, "My desire is to depart and be with Christ, for that is far better." In 2 Corinthians 5:8, Paul states, "We would rather be away from the body and at home with the Lord." This is not the final state of the Christian believer: It is intermediate, the soul is bodiless, heaven is not yet, and the resurrection of the body has yet to take place. But there is a real sense in which the soul is "with Christ," although so far as life on this earth is concerned, the state is accurately described as being one of "sleep."

What of the unsaved, the unrighteous dead? They, too, have passed into hades where they wait, bodiless and conscious. We have referred already to the "great gulf fixed," and we read that the rich man of Luke 16:24 was in a state of conscious suffering. In 2 Peter 2:9 we are further told: "The Lord knows how to rescue the godly from trial, and to keep the unrighteous under punishment until the day of judgment."

This state of waiting ends at the second advent, to which reference has already been made in the chapter on "How Will the World End?" The visible and glorious appearing of our Lord Jesus Christ brings all earthly history to an end; it is the climax and fulfillment of life in both states. Christ is Lord of the universe and holds "the keys of Death and Hades" (Revelation 1:18). His coming means the end of this space-time world and of all material and mortal existence.

The second advent issues immediately in the resurrection of the dead, which means that the bodiless souls in hades will be "clothed" with new resurrection bodies and that the living on earth ("we who are alive, who are left," 1 Thessalonians 4:17) will be transformed, the mortal into the immortal body, "in the twinkling of an eye" (1 Corinthians 15:52). 1 Corinthians 15 is the great passage here and repays careful reading. It begins with the marshaling of evidence for our Lord's own resurrection, goes on to state emphatically, "But in fact Christ has been raised from the dead, the first fruits of those who have fallen asleep," and continues with a discussion on the question, "How are the dead raised? With what manner of body do they come?"

We are told that there is a definite order of events in the resurrection and that the raising and transformation of the faithful precedes that of unbelievers (v. 23), although *all* are raised irrespective of their goodness or badness (v. 22). It is particularly important to notice that the resurrection of the body does not mean the resuscitation of the flesh (v. 50), for there is a distinction drawn between the words "body" and "flesh." The argument of this chapter should be noted carefully, and it will be seen that Paul uses a number of illuminating analogies to make clear the connection between the former body of our earthly state and the body of resurrection. There is identity and there is also transformation; the new is not the old resuscitated, but transformed.

Eventually all will stand before the tribunal of Christ, where will take place judgment of both individuals and societies. "For we must all appear before the judgment seat of Christ" (2 Corinthians 5:10, written to Christian believers); "The men of Nineveh will arise at the judgment with this generation and condemn it" (Matthew 12:41). The criterion of judgment is clearly laid down; it is faith issuing in good works, or, as Paul expresses it, "faith active in love" (Moffatt). Christ himself is on the throne, and the decisive factor will be our relationship to him. Sin is primarily a wrong relationship to Christ, which has issued in evil deeds. The teaching of Jesus is very clear that the judgment divides all beings into two groups: saved and lost, sheep and goats, wheat and tares. We have no grounds at all for expecting that there will be a large, vague, and indeterminate body of people who are neither on one side nor the other.

We can be sure that God will act in perfect justice and that there will be different degrees of responsibility. It will be more tolerable in that day for Sodom than for the cities which knew Christ (Luke 10:12), as there will be differences of guilt and differences therefore of punishment (Luke 12:47-48). It is idle to ask, "What about the heathen who have never heard of Christ?" because we are assured that no man will be judged beyond the light he has received. It is of far greater importance to ask ourselves how far we have responded to the privileges of a land of plentiful Bibles and open churches.

The final destiny of the wicked is *hell,* a word which, as we have already pointed out, should not be confused with *hades.* It was Jesus himself, the Son of God, who used such terms as "lost" and "perish." While it is easy for our conceptions of hell to become crude and materialistic, there is no doubt that Jesus knew and taught that some terrible fate awaited the willful and unrepentant sinner.

Heaven, the final destiny of those who are saved, is, in substance, to be with Christ and like Christ. It is symbolized as a city or a perfect community where there is fellowship with God and unspoiled holiness. A detailed description is beyond all human imagination and understanding, and materialistic attempts are usually far from attractive. We know, however, that a realm where Christ is in complete control and where his Presence fills everyone and everything must mean the very height of bliss. Here on earth is our opportunity to make sure that we share in the glory there.

But we conclude by repeating that no one need wait until after death to experience the reality of heaven. We can know it in part now. Paul, writing to the Christians in Philippi, which was a Roman colony, said, "We are a colony of heaven" (3:20, Moffatt); we are in foreign territory, but we are already citizens of the eternal world. "God gave [past, not future tense] us eternal life, and this life is in his Son. He who has the Son has life; he who has not the Son has not life" (1 John 5:11-12). Could anything be clearer!

*There seem to be so many "decent people" in the world who never dream of calling themselves Christians. They never read the Bible or go to church; yet their lives are honest, straightforward, and attractive. Why bother such people with complicated doctrines? Are they not far more Christian in character than many so-called Christians? Surely the important thing is to be sincere in one's beliefs, and it cannot much matter what a man believes so long as he is sincere.*

# 16

## Are Decency and Sincerity Enough?

A problem which bothers many Christian people arises from the fact that there appear to be so many decent, good-living men and women in the world who do not claim to be Christians. They never go to church or read the Bible, and they live their lives altogether apart from organized religion. Why offer such people the gospel? Surely the essential thing is to live a good life. As long as these folk are kind and helpful to their fellowmen and do not bring any harm to anybody else, what more is required?

The problem sometimes takes a rather different form. Does it matter what a man believes provided that he is sincere? Sincerity, like decency, makes for attractive character. There are numbers of people who, although not professing Christians, are nevertheless sincere in the opinions they hold. There are times when we are tempted to turn impatiently from creeds and doctrines and to agree with those who insist that it is the life alone which counts, that it cannot matter what we believe, so long as we believe it sincerely.

We propose in this chapter to examine more closely both of these problems, and first of all to suggest reasons why sincerity of belief is not enough. To begin with, it is possible to be sincerely in error, as a few simple illustrations will show. Think of a child in a Congo village suffering from acute appendicitis. The natives, who sincerely believe that the trouble is due to a wicked spirit, gather round and beat their drums in order to drive the spirit away. But the child dies. The natives were all desperately sincere, but they were wrong. Their sincerity could neither effect a cure nor alter the fatal result.

Truth and accuracy, not just sincerity, are what matter. A man may drive into a stream because the glint of the moon has made it look like a road, but his good intentions will not save him from a ducking or worse. The invalid who drinks from the bottle of disinfectant carelessly left by his bedside, supposing that he is taking a healing draught of medicine, dies. Sincerity has not saved him. This fact, that men can be sincerely deluded, can be sincerely in error, needs stressing because we take risks and expose ourselves to dangers in regard to our religious beliefs (or lack of beliefs) which we would never countenance in other departments of life.

Moreover, character is the direct result of belief. People whose beliefs are wrong, act wrongly. Nazi morality, of which we have heard and seen such appalling examples, was the outcome of Nazi ideology. When men reach a fixed conviction that they belong to a master race, they will show by their conduct how revoltingly others can be treated as inferiors. In an interesting study, Dr. W. E. Sangster has shown how Adolf Hitler, according to some commonly accepted standards of "respectable" morality, could be regarded as decent and sincere. He was a nonsmoker, more or less temperate in his habits, and reasonably kind to children. But he believed certain things which set the world ablaze and burnt to the ground the peace and happiness of millions. Plainly it does matter what a man believes.

If this fact is still in dispute, then why is it that conduct differs so widely in, say, an Indian village and an English village? Why do Mohammedans treat their womenfolk as inferiors? Again, why do Marxists act so differently from Christians? If one man says, "I believe that money is the most important thing in life," and another says, "I believe that friendship is the most important"—then they will soon draw apart in character; they are different men.

It will be rightly assumed from the foregoing that we are claiming that Christian character is the result of Christian belief. Yet just here is the real problem. How is it that many people seem to have a Christian character without Christian belief? The answer is partly that they have been brought up in a Christian tradition and environment which has power-fully influenced them, even if indirectly and unconsciously. As they are living on a tradition to which they now contribute little or nothing, it is not being too severe to say that they are spiritual parasites. A man who is a complete idler might live for a time on the financial capital left to him by his father; "the father planted the apple trees, and the son is content to pass the applesauce."

It is possible to live *for a time* a morally upright life on the faith of others, a faith which we no longer share. But a sharp reminder is needed that this spiritual capital, the Chris-tian tradition of Western civilization, is now practically ex-hausted. Thank God for every "decent person" about us. But whence this Christian morality? How great are the debts owed by both nation and individual to parents and grand-parents who held definite convictions!

There is another answer to the problem which arises from the existence of Christian character without, apparently, any basis in Christian belief. Happily, a man's real beliefs—the convictions by which he lives—do not always correspond to his theoretical beliefs. It is an encouraging thought that much of the good character which cheers us as we go about the world does rest upon strong conviction of the heart, even though this has never been openly acknowledged.

We return now to the other main question: Why is it not sufficient to live an average, decent sort of life? We have already seen how spineless and feeble character without conviction can be. It is possible to be good—for nothing—to maintain a way of life which is negative, or at least, passive. Our Lord's parables were most insistent on this, and in them people were condemned for not living positively. The one-talent man was probably "decent," but his sin consisted in failing to use gainfully what had first been given to him by God. Similarly, the wicked of Matthew 25 who were "cursed" by the King had not done anything wrong—or right. They had just done nothing.

Real goodness is creative, positive, and dynamic; it is life with a purpose. The benefactors of mankind have been men with crusading hearts who believed in a cause that was right and who were prepared to make sacrifices to achieve its success. When a man becomes a Christian, that means he is called of God to the achievement of something; and he who hesitates at the sound of the call hears the solemn words, "He who is not with me is against me; and he who does not gather with me scatters."

Is it really true that any man is, in fact, "decent"? Judged by the standards of outward action and social convention, perhaps we may answer "Yes"; but what of the inner life? In his Sermon on the Mount the Lord Jesus taught that God's laws applied there no less, that hatred was murder, lust was adultery, and that no man was clean within. The writings of a psychologist like Jung have shown what frightful indecency is in the heart of every man.

Are pride and self-righteousness any less sins because they are respectable? The fundamental sin is to ignore the claims of God. It is not simply a question of what we consider to be sufficient, but of what God has declared to be necessary. Is it honest to enjoy the hard-won liberties which have come from an open Bible and then neglect its message today? Remember, "decency" crucified Christ. Not the publicans and the harlots of the city, but those who were socially respectable acted together to bring about the death of God's Son. In an earlier chapter we quoted more fully the words of Dr. James Stewart in this connection when he wrote, "Jesus was crucified by the ordinary sins of every day." Self-interest, fear, anger, and spite—these are so commonplace that many people would scarcely regard them as sins at all. They certainly would not allow them to interfere with a man's reputation for social uprightness and conformity. Might not this "decency," then, be another name for self-righteousness and pride?

Calvary exposes the real state of our hearts and delivers us from both sin's guilt and power. Sincerity and decency are not enough. God has been at pains to reveal the truth to us, and the final revelation of what is good and true is seen at the cross. It is Christ alone who is made unto us "our wisdom, our righteousness and sanctification and redemption."

*This has always been a profound mystery. There seems to be so much unnecessary suffering in the world, and it is difficult for some people to reconcile the idea of a God of love with so much that is unjust and cruel. Is there any purpose in suffering? Or are we just victims of circumstances? Does the Christian faith shed any light on the problem of pain?*

# 17

## Why Does God Permit Suffering?

Let us admit at the outset that no simple or complete answer can be given to this question. The problem of suffering always has been a problem. If God is good, men have argued, how can he permit the almost indescribable horrors that have afflicted the history of mankind? It has even been suggested that God, like a cruel father who enjoys the spectacle of his children suffering, stands aside and makes no effort to help. Now while no complete answer can be given to a question which to some extent must always remain a mystery, the Christian faith does afford valuable insights. There are definite clues in the Bible and the Christian faith to show that suffering is not meaningless.

To begin with, there is no problem at all unless we believe in the existence of a God who is good. This is an obvious presupposition. The African who lives his life in constant fear of spirits believes in many gods who are malevolent. To him therefore there is no problem of quite this kind; he might resignedly conclude, as Gloucester expresses it in *King Lear:*

As flies to wanton boys, are we to the gods;
They kill us for their sport.

But if the assumption is made that God is good, the questioner finds it hard to reconcile with this the existence of so much pain in the world around. Here we must stress a fact equally evident, that belief in God's goodness grew up alongside man's experience of pain. So far from hindering belief in God, suffering has frequently caused it to grow.

In fact, claiming that it is suffering most of all which has led many people to believe in God would be no exaggeration. In some mysterious way, suffering has not destroyed but strengthened faith. Living through the horrors of the concentration camp during World War II, a German pastor read again and again the Book of Job. Why this particular book? Job presents a picture of intense suffering, yet its effect upon the reader is to give reassurance of God's majesty and love. Faith is not injured but inspired.

We can therefore speak guardedly of the value of pain. In a previous chapter, "What Is the Purpose of the World?" it was argued that this world is a "vale of soul making." Pain has its part to play in this same purpose. Suppose, for the moment, we put the question the other way round, trying to imagine what the world would be like if God did *not* permit suffering. Think of the virtues that would be lost—patience, endurance, fortitude, and self-sacrifice. Full beauty and development of Christian character would be impossible, for the possibility of suffering has to be included as an essential ingredient. A pearl is the way an oyster deals with the grit beneath its shell. In like ways are pearls of character produced. Shakespeare's tragedies, like *Hamlet* and *Othello,* revealing, as they do, the innermost feelings of men and women, demonstrate the greatness and refinement of character that result from suffering.

Pain also helps us to avoid more serious physical ills. We soon learn that it is harmful to hit our thumb instead of the nail with a hammer! Pain becomes a necessary discipline in the safeguarding of bodily health. Think, too, of the extent to which suffering has proved a spur to progress. Medical and scientific discoveries, not to mention great social reforms, have often been inspired by the necessity of facing this very problem. Are we not then justified in making the claim that suffering is not meaningless, but that it does possess a definite value?

If these considerations still leave much suffering unexplained, then there are other points to be made. The world as we see it today is not as God intended it to be. In chapter 3, "What Is Wrong with the World?" we pointed out that man was originally created in perfection to be a child of God, but that he is now a fallen creature. There has been rebellion in the world; therefore, conditions are not as God would have them, and not as they will ultimately be remade. If we tamper with God's laws for righteous and happy living, then painful clashes are inevitable.

Illustrations of this are so obvious that we need scarcely take up space with them. People in many nations are suffering from the desolation brought about by war. Who is responsible? Is it God? Does God take pleasure in the self-seeking, the covetousness, the lying, and the cruelty that issue in so much pain? We need to reread the words of James, which are as relevant today in their sound common sense as when they were written: "What causes wars, and what causes fightings among you? Is it not your passions that are at war in your members? You desire and do not have; so you kill. And you covet and cannot obtain. . . ." It is nonsense to suggest that these sins have been exclusive to any nation. A war itself may be over, but we all persist in those very sins that lead to war.

Furthermore, man is a social creature, and it is his lot to share in the misfortunes, as well as the blessings, that come the way of all mankind. We do not live our lives in isolation; no man can sin to himself. The world is a community, and strife in one of its corners affects us all. The drunkard may suffer for his evil indulgence, but it will probably be his wife and children who suffer most. There are diseases in the world today which have been produced by sin on a racial scale. God may use suffering, which he has not himself caused, to correct and recall men from the folly of evil.

When we turn to the words of Jesus, we find there a full acknowledgment of the fact that this is a world of suffering, that there will be a constant strife and tension between the forces of good and evil in the world, and that these have their issue in pain. And no one knew the mind of God as did God's Son. These are among his pronouncements on the subject: "In the world you have tribulation"; "Blessed are you when men revile you and persecute you"; "If any man would come after me, let him deny himself and take up his cross and follow me." To be a real Christian, then, certainly does not mean an escape from suffering.

It is important to notice that Jesus was far more concerned about sin than pain. As always, he went to the heart of things; but we have shifted the emphasis, and our problem is rather one of pain. Obviously, if being a Christian did mean escape from suffering, then multitudes would want to become Christians for this reason alone. But what kind of Christians would they be? The word would be emptied of any real content, and God's great purpose among men, the creation of Christlike lives, would fail.

The main answer to the question is—God himself *shares* our suffering. He is not a disinterested spectator, or even an impotent admirer—he is in this problem with us. Can anything be ultimately evil in which God so intimately shares?

Paul said that his ambition was to "know him . . . and the *fellowship of his sufferings*" (Revised Version—italics added); elsewhere he wrote, "I rejoice in my sufferings for your sake, and in my flesh I complete what is lacking in Christ's afflictions." The God we worship is the God who, at the cross, was in Christ reconciling the world unto himself. Through suffering God has been able to reveal himself and to accomplish something in the hearts and lives of men that would never have been possible without it. The sorrows of Hosea and Jeremiah were foreshadowings of the passion of Christ. Pain is hard to bear when it seems devoid of meaning and purpose; then we gaze at the cross, and meaning and purpose are there.

No one has any right to deny that suffering is worthwhile without examining its outcome in the future. We speak of the life to come (which was discussed more fully in chapter 15) with some hesitancy in this connection because of the common objection that the Christian answer to this world's sorrows is "pie in the sky when you die." This is very far from being the case, and we have sought to show that pain has a real meaning for this life; but if, as we confidently believe, there is a life beyond, then present suffering must be estimated against that eternal background.

Paul contrasted his present "light affliction" with future bliss. "For this slight momentary affliction," he wrote, "is preparing us for an eternal weight of glory beyond all comparison." The Christian believes in a world where there are no more tears, but eternal life for him is not simply a life that begins after physical death. He begins to possess it as soon as he becomes a Christian and is therefore able to judge its equality here and now. It is admitted that much suffering is meaningless apart from this fact of eternal life, but the Christian is prepared to assert with Paul that events here on earth are but the birth pangs of a new world: "I consider that the sufferings of this present time are not worth comparing with the glory that is to be revealed to us."

A lady whose life radiates joy was once talking to a friend about suffering. The latter said, "You speak about suffering as if you believed in it." "Yes, I do," she replied, "nearly everything worthwhile that I have learned in life came to me through pain." If it is possible to realize this even in our present life (as we shall certainly know it more completely in that which is to come), then the problem of suffering ceases to be a dark and meaningless mystery.

*There are those who admire Christ and who believe that there is much that is good and worthwhile in the Christian religion, yet who feel that the church just does not appeal to them. They say that they have no time for organized religion. They claim to worship God in their own way. They say that there are lots of hypocrites in the church, as well as much unnecessary machinery. Can't one be just as good a Christian without going to church?*

# 18

## Can One Be a Christian Without Going to Church?

The philosophers of the Middle Ages often used to argue the question, "How many parts can you take away from a sheep, and it still remain a sheep?" In our modern age it might be more fitting to apply the question to an automobile. How many parts can you take away from a car, and it still remain a car? Fenders are not necessary, a horn is not essential, seats are a luxury, and it is possible to dispense with brakes. Can we remove the plugs or the carburetor? At some point in this process the car ceases to be a going concern. But even before that point is reached, what a poor car it would be!

How many "parts" can you take away from a Christian, and he still remain a Christian? Is baptism necessary, or Bible reading? Perhaps personal witness is an optional extra, and some people try to dispense with the Lord's Supper. At some point in the process it is impossible to continue the claim that we are discussing a Christian at all. But long before that point is reached—what a poor Christian, anyway!

How foolish it is to attempt to be an "irreducible mini-mum" type of Christian! "It is fitting for us to fulfill all righteousness," to go the whole way with the Lord Jesus Christ. So, even if it were possible to be a Christian apart from the church (which we deny), it is certainly not possible to be a full Christian. Should one desire anything less than that? "But," someone will protest, "is it essential to a full Christian life that I should belong to a church? I can pray daily and read my Bible at home; I can live a Christian life and serve Christ in the common ways of life—all without going to church. And who dare say that I am not a Christian?"

"Read your Bible," did you say? When you get to Genesis 12, you will be reading about the foundation of the church; and from there onwards throughout the whole of the Old Testament and the New you will continue to read its developing story. You will still be reading about it when you reach the last chapter of the last book, for "the Spirit and the Bride [i.e., the church] say, 'Come' " (Revelation 22:17). How, then, can you read and love the book which is all about the church of God and yet stay outside it?

There are, however, those who say, "Yes, we quite agree that a Christian must be part of the church of God, part of the whole church, the universal church. But surely one can belong to *the* church without belonging to *a* church; one can be part of the redeemed community, militant on earth and triumphant in heaven, without belonging to any local assembly of Christians."

Now, this implied distinction between the church and a church, between the universal church and the local church, as if they were two different things, is altogether misleading and false. The local church is the universal church in that particular place. The universal church on earth is not some airy, invisible, disembodied entity to which one belongs "in

spirit." It is "the church of God which is at Corinth" (2 Corinthians 1:1), at Philippi, at Sydney, at Omaha. Certainly
it is "the church of God," the one universal, apostolic church
founded by the Lord Jesus Christ, but it is also at a particular
place. We often talk about "the churches" in the plural, and
this scriptural phrase has reference to the fact that the one
church assembles in many places. But there is, in fact, only
one church, appearing at this place and at that. Let us, then,
beware of this false antithesis.

"But," it will be objected further, "what about an invalid
confined permanently to bed, or a Christian youth alone
in the armed forces, or a missionary isolated in an animistic
village? These cannot go to a church, but surely they can
and do belong to the universal church?" The answer is that
these Christians do belong to a local church, or to a com-
munion of such churches. A person does not cease to be
a member of a community merely because he is separated
geographically from it. I am a member of the local church
on a Sunday morning at 11 A.M. when we are assembled
for worship; I am no less a member on Monday morning
at 11 A.M. when I am alone at the office.

John was alone on the island of Patmos, geographically
isolated. But he was a very live member of the church—yes,
and of the local churches of Asia Minor in which he was an
elder. There is all the difference in the world between geo-
graphical separation and spiritual separation, cutting oneself
off through pride and self-sufficiency. The invalid confined
to bed is not like the person who says, "I have no need of
you" (1 Corinthians 12:21), and we probably know such
Christians who are very real members of the local church.

The local church, then, is the universal church in a particular place; they are not two, but one. We may now proceed to the main reasons why it is essential to belong to
"the church of God at ——."

1. The church is an essential part of the purpose of God. It is clearly revealed in Scripture that the purpose of God is to make his salvation known to the whole human race through a redeemed community. In the Old Testament this people of God, this elect race, this holy nation, this royal priesthood, is called Israel. Founded with the call of Abraham, redeemed at the Passover and the Red Sea, brought into covenant relationship with God at Sinai, Israel's election was for her a vocation—the vocation of bringing the knowledge of the true God and his salvation to all men. When disobedient to this vocation, God sent to Israel the long line of prophets and, last of all, his beloved Son. But the strategy of God was still the same—salvation through a holy people.

So it was, that at the beginning of his ministry, with the call of the apostles, Jesus began to create the new Israel, the church. At the time of the first great confession of faith, he at once made the significant declaration: "On this rock ['You are the Christ, the Son of the living God'] I will build my church." This he did through his atoning work on the cross, through his glorious resurrection, and the gift of the Spirit at Pentecost. Jesus lived, died, and rose again to create the church (Ephesians 5:25), which is his body, in order that the manifold wisdom of God might be made known through the church (Ephesians 3:10). This is the purpose of God, and to be within the purpose of God, it is necessary to be within the community of God.

2. The church is essential to the Christian, because the Christian life is by nature corporate and communal. When we think of the Christian life, what picture have we in mind? Look at two New Testament pictures: a vine and its branches, a body and its members. Christ is the heavenly vine (the Old Testament figure for Israel), and Christians are the branches, sharing a common life in him. Christ is

the body, and we are the members; in him we are organically related, nourished by the common life-stream of the Holy Spirit. A separate branch, or a separate member, is—dead.

The great New Testament phrase "in Christ" is both personal and communal, as may be seen from the fact that the phrase "in the body" is sometimes substituted for it. (Compare Galatians 3:27 and 1 Corinthians 12:13.) But where do we find an isolated, separated Christian in the New Testament? And as a matter of practical interest, do you really know any vital Christians apart from the community— this community of Christ?

3. The world can be evangelized only through the church. Apart from the Christian community, who would translate, print, and distribute the Holy Scriptures? Who would teach the young and be responsible for religious education? Who would send out and support missionaries? Who would preach and broadcast the gospel? Who would make any impact upon organized social evils? In a word, who would carry on the manifold ministry of Christ? Could unrelated individuals, even if they would, do this work? Do Christians(?) who avoid the church actually accept and shoulder these responsibilities? History and experience give an unmistakable answer to this question.

Of all people the Christian should be sensible and practical. It is not good enough to be vague and nebulous, to feel a mystical and sentimental loyalty to an invisible and intangible church. Christ came in flesh and blood—visible, concrete, local. In the church is where we belong and where we must serve. If "Christ loved the church and gave himself up for her," then we, too, must love as he loved and give up our lives in her service.